D0849078

Allan Seager

Twayne's United States Authors Series

Warren French, Editor

Indiana University, Indianapolis

TUSAS 446

ALLAN SEAGER
(1906–1968)
Photograph by Lusha Nelson
Courtesy of Jane Lehac

Allan Seager

By Stephen E. Connelly

Indiana State University

Twayne Publishers • Boston

Allan Seager

Stephen E. Connelly

Copyright © 1983 by G. K. Hall & Company
All Rights Reserved
Published by Twayne Publishers
A Division of G. K. Hall & Company
70 Lincoln Street
Boston, Massachusetts 02111

Book Production by Marne B. Sultz
Book Design by Barbara Anderson

Printed on permanent/durable acid-free
paper and bound in the United States of
America.

Library of Congress Cataloging in Publication Data

Connelly, Stephen E.
Allan Seager.

(Twayne's United States authors series; TUSAS 446)
Bibliography: p. 116
Includes index.
1. Seager, Allan, 1906–1968—Criticism and
interpretation.   I. Title.   II. Series
PS3537.E123Z63   1983   813'.54   82-23416
ISBN 0-8057-7386-X

To My Father, My Mother, My Sister, My Wife, My Children:
Dia anseo isteach!

Contents

About the Author

Stephen Connelly is Associate Professor of English at Indiana State University. He has degrees from the University of Michigan (B.A., M.A.) and Indiana University (Ph. D.). His publications include articles on James Joyce, Philip José Farmer, Uncle Scrooge, and Handball in Ireland. He developed and teaches an introductory literature course for the Hoosier Schoolmaster Radio Series. He is currently Editor of Theses and Dissertations for the School of Graduate Studies and Book Review Editor of *The Journal of Mind and Behavior*.

Preface

Allan Seager is one of those shadowy figures, "the minor writer," whose neglect at the hands of both public and critics has been many times lamented but never remedied. Seager's relative obscurity a little over a decade after his death is difficult to explain, for the reasons are numerous and complex. Chief among them, though, is sheer bad luck: a wartime paper shortage ended *Equinox*'s stay on the best-seller lists; *Death of Anger* hit print just as internal squabbles were destroying the firm that published it; *The Glass House* ran up against an intractable literary widow and suffered extended excision and revision.

Seager's lack of popularity is also attributable, to a certain extent, to his deliberate artistic choices. In an age of form he insisted upon emphasizing ideas. He was in many ways too old-fashioned to be fashionable, for his attempts to write a twentieth-century American novel of manners invoke the great nineteenth-century novels. His concern for personal dignity made impossible the self-publicity so often important to the success of his contemporaries. And he chose his "field," the Midwest and the middle class, quite aware that the so-called "midwestern novel" rarely received acclaim. His notes show that he knew he risked neglect in his choices of subject matter and form, but he made his artistic choices consciously, and they were made by a fine intelligence.

Allan Seager's work does have some persuasive admirers. Hugh Kenner called him "as good a novelist as America had" during the period in which he wrote, and Malcolm Cowley wrote me that Seager was "perhaps the outstanding example of the gifted writer more or less overlooked because he didn't belong to a group or cult and because he lived far from New York or San Francisco." James Dickey's high regard for Seager was made a matter of public record in a 1968 *Esquire* article; other novelists and poets, such as Robert Penn Warren, Anton Myrer, Carl Sandburg, and Donald Hall have praised Seager highly. The list is more extensive, but such a list, no matter how eminent the persons on it, does not qualify a writer for greatness. Seager would have been the first to scorn the suggestion that it did: his novels demonstrate his aversion to the Madison Avenue testimonial approach to fame. But this wholehearted admiration by individuals of demonstrated critical acumen is honest evidence that an odd gap exists between Allan Seager's worth and the public recognition he has received.

Any rise in Seager's reputation as a writer will no doubt be a gradual and long-term process. This study, at best, could be little more than a small beginning, and it is intended only as a general introduction to Seager's work: his themes and motifs, his great concern for the quality of life in America, and the sense of responsibility from which he wrote. Seager believed that it was impossible to separate art from the artist. In the working notes to a novel left unfinished at his death he wrote, "In a sense any novel is autobiographical. How can it not be?" Of necessity, then, this study begins with his life and refers to it often. Finally, it is clear that Seager was most serious as a novelist; it was in his novels that he attempted to say all that he "wanted said." Consequently, this study focuses primarily upon his novels.

Stephen E. Connelly

Indiana State University

Acknowledgments

I am grateful to Joan Seager Fry for permission to quote from *Amos Berry* (New York: Simon and Schuster, 1953), *Death of Anger* (New York: McDowell, Obolensky, 1960), *Equinox* (New York: Simon and Schuster, 1943), *A Frieze of Girls* (New York: McGraw-Hill, 1964), *The Glass House* (New York: McGraw-Hill, 1968), *Hilda Manning* (New York: Simon and Schuster, 1956), *The Inheritance* (New York: Simon and Schuster, 1948), *Memoirs of a Tourist* (Evanston: Northwestern University Press, 1962), *The Old Man of the Mountain* (New York: Simon and Schuster, 1950), and *They Worked For a Better World* (New York: Macmillan, 1939). I am also deeply indebted to Joan Seager Fry for providing me with early drafts of some of Allan Seager's fiction, unpublished stories, diverse notes, photographs, leads, insights, addresses, and above all for her patience in answering my questions—in a manner always witty and pleasurable.

I am grateful to Jane Sherman Lehac for providing the frontispiece. I owe Mrs. Lehac a great deal of thanks, as well, for the notes and letters she has loaned me, for the detailed account of Seager's *Vanity Fair* years, for her perpetual inspiration, and for eight years of aid and comfort.

I am indebted to Earl Karr, Louella Reynolds, Jane Warner, Donald Hall, Laura Baddeley, Rita Blake, James Goodrich, and the Reverend Dr. W. J. Hampton for granting me lengthy and informative interviews.

I am obligated to Helen Rudolphi Tremble, Sheridan Baker, Knox Burger, Anton Myrer, Hugh Whitney Morrison, and Hugh Kenner, all of whom loaned me letters of Seager's, and all of whom were most generous in supplying information. I thank Phil Wikelund for helping me start, and Jon Bracker for help with research in the Bay Area.

I am grateful to the Humanities Research Center, the University of Texas at Austin, for permission to quote from Seager's correspondence with Edmund Blunden.

I am grateful to the Mugar Memorial Library and its Director, Dr. Howard Gottlieb, for permission to quote from the "Working Notebook for *Equinox*" in the Allan Seager Collection, Department of Special Collections, Boston University Libraries.

I am especially grateful to the Bancroft Library of the University of California at Berkeley for permission to quote from materials in the

Allan Seager Collection and also for the kind help of the Bancroft staff. I must thank Indiana State University for the Faculty Research Grant which helped defray the costs of early research in the Bancroft Library.

Thanks to Pam for proofreading and for advice. Thanks to Kathy and Sean for understanding.

Chronology

1968 Marries Joan Rambo. May 10, dies in St. Joseph's Hospital,
      Ann Arbor. *The Glass House: The Life of Theodore Roethke* pub-
      lished posthumously.

Chapter One
The Life

Early Influences: Rooted and Uprooted

John Braithwaite Allan Seager was born February 5, 1906, in Adrian, Michigan. In few states has the clash and mesh of frontier and industrial America been so spectacular, and in few places have they coexisted so uneasily for so long. Allan Seager was born within one hundred miles of Detroit, the automobile manufacturing center of the world, and though during his lifetime he witnessed the northward retreat of the hunter's and fisherman's paradise, he was also within a hundred miles of Hemingway's Big Two-Hearted River. He grew up with the state's decidedly dual heritage, and he watched as industrialization grew strong at the expense of the frontier spirit: the heritage of the trappers, lumbermen, and farmers.

When he died in 1968, Seager's home was in Tecumseh, Michigan, barely ten miles from his birthplace. Allan Seager could not escape from Lenawee County in either his life or his art, for his roots were extremely deep in the area in which he was born, just as they were deep in America. His great-great-grandfather Elijah Seger (*sic*) fought in the American War for Independence, and these Segers were among Vermont's early settlers. Elijah's son Aaron married Rebecca Harrison, a cousin of President Benjamin Harrison. Allan Seager's grandfather, Beauman Seager, was among the first settlers in Lenawee County, Michigan, and he fought with the Union Army in the Civil War. Sitting at Beauman's knee as a young boy, Seager heard a matter-of-fact account of the Battle of Gettysburg. As a boy he also read the three volumes of his maternal grandfather, John B. Allan's, Civil War diaries.

The energy and involvement of his family in America's history impressed him even then. Young Allan overheard tales of the family's early years in Lenawee County, not only the tales of Beauman Seager, but also those of the relatives such as the Reynoldses, who furnished the county with its first Secretary and who, especially in the person of Harold Reynolds, personified the basic duality of the state's heritage: Harold was a lumberman, one of an already dying breed whose end was hastened by Henry Ford.

The past was kept alive in the Seager family. For Allan Seager the histories of Michigan and the United States were not mere textbook matter, or legend, or bright pretty tales. Rather they were part of being a Seager, inextricably tied up with the family's history. Seager's past, like Faulkner's, was neither something that had passed nor that could be escaped. Its presence was stamped upon his mind by the strong old man who re-created Gettysburg and by the strong uncles who re-created the early wilderness of Lenawee County. Because his own roots were so deep, because the past was alive for him, Seager could see the influence of his heritage upon himself and his family, and he believed he could see its influence upon those around him who were ignorant of it. Little wonder he repeatedly examined in his fiction the influence of the land and its history upon the men who inhabit it.

A high board fence with a gate in the middle ran behind the Seager house in Adrian. The gate was not for the convenience of the Seager family, but for local mill workers who otherwise would have been forced some distance out of their way to get to work. As a very young boy Allan Seager liked to be home to watch as the workers went to work or returned home; his lifelong habit of observing people was formed early, almost ingrained. The gate also taught a lesson in local responsibility and obligations to one's neighbors that Seager explored in his fiction to the end of his life.

Arch Seager, Allan's father, traveled widely for the Peerless Wire and Fence Company, at that time one of the largest fence companies in the nation, and his ability as a sales representative was almost legendary. His travels took him through the whole Mississippi Valley, and his returns home were grand occasions. He brought tales of his travels, as well as tales collected during them, including descriptions of all classes of people and most of the Midwest, earning him a reputation as an expert storyteller that survives today. Sherwood Anderson once exchanged tales with Arch Seager well into the early morning hours and subsequently wrote in a letter to Allan: "If you have any talent, it comes from him."[1]

While his father may have provided him with a love for the story, his mother, Emma Allan Seager, provided something just as valuable. She was responsible for most of the actual rearing of Allan and his sister, Jane, because of the frequent and extended absences of his father. Allan was a precocious reader who began reading very young, books that were "much advanced for his age." This impulse to read was probably implanted by his mother, who read to Allan and Jane often and for great lengths of time, seated between them on an oversized leather chair. Emma Seager did more than just read to her young son; she always took time to answer his questions, to explain words or passages that he did not understand. It didn't matter what she was doing: housecleaning, dishes, ironing—they could all wait; her son's questions, his education, were more important. No book in the house was off limits. Learning took precedence over matters that Seager soon noticed were viewed by other parents in other households as more pressing than a child's questions. Allan was promoted to the second grade before he had half finished the first. It is hardly surprising that he always regarded education as a continual process not to be confined to classrooms.

From among his friends acquaintances, two Allan Seagers emerge. One is reserved: the observer, the thinker, the reader, the scholar. The other is outgoing: the storyteller, the *raconteur*, the witty social being who could so dominate a conversation that it seemed to turn into a monologue. In the persons of his mother and father, then, the impulses that shaped Seager's life and writing were there from the beginning. Both impulses received impetus from other sources.

When Seager was nearly eleven, his father was transferred to the Memphis branch of Peerless Wire and Fence, and the family with roots so deep in Michigan was suddenly uprooted and transplanted in alien, Southern soil. Seager resisted. He was so angered by the move that he vowed to make no friends in school; he vowed, in fact, not to speak to schoolmates, a vow central to his short story, "Flight South."

Seager stubbornly stuck to his vow despite the best efforts of his parents to draw him out. An immediate result was that he assumed the role of observer almost exclusively, a role that served him to the end of his life, and into which he would occasionally slide almost automatically. A second result of the move was the cultivation of Seager's swimming ability, a talent which played a part in his attaining a Rhodes Scholarship at Michigan. After nearly a year of his silence and loneliness, Seager's parents made him a member of the YMCA, hoping he would make friends there. Seager protected his solitude by swimming constantly, hating even to sit on the side and rest, because he would be vulnerable to conversation.

He became an excellent swimmer. When he began to enter and win local races, he was thrust into the limelight, hastening the relaxation of his vow. He understood, at last, that he did want to be accepted; and though he was accepted and eventually made a number of lifelong friends, he considered himself an outsider in the South. He was thus the beneficiary of something he later declared important to budding writers, an extra-environmental perspective.

Seager's vow yielded another predictable return, time on his hands. To employ it, he zealously pursued a path he was already on: he read with increasing intensity. After relaxing the vow, he continued his voracious reading. Early in high school he set himself goals, a one-hundred page per day minimum at one point. Later he promised himself to read eight hours a day after his shift in a Memphis box factory. A partial list of one summer's reading reveals the seriousness of his intent: "Las Bas, Les Diaboliques, Nietzsche, A Rebours, Nostromo, Hippolyte Taine's History, Baudelaire, Salambo, Dreiser, Flaubert, Ibsen, Cashel Byron's Profession, Drieser's Genius, Dostoevsky, Merimee, Stendahl, de Goncourt (*sic*)."[2]

He not only read widely, but by January 1, 1924, he had begun keeping a steady diary. He tried to write daily, a discipline continued to the end of his life and suspended only when he was hard at work on a book. Thirty years later his early notebooks became *A Frieze of Girls*. Seager's self-imposed isolation gave his literary career the impetus of the discipline essential to a writer. Discipline was, in fact, always a basic virtue in his eyes, just as regimentation was a basic evil.

During the Memphis years the passion to become a writer seized Seager, no doubt from a combination of such things as his love of reading, the admiration for the tale implanted in his childhood, an inborn sensitivity, and practiced observation. Writing is a craft practiced in isolation, yet its results are so public that anyone may view them: it dovetailed neatly with Seager's own dual nature.

Not only did Seager begin to write in Memphis, he also became engaged there in the other chief pursuit of his life, teaching. He gave swimming lessons at the Y, and he helped educate his sister Jane. His impulse to teach was lifelong, culminating in his distinguished teaching career at the University of Michigan. Seager carefully guided Jane's reading, making lists so that she wouldn't waste her time on trash. The year before she entered Episcopal High School in Memphis, Seager decided Jane would be the first freshman to win the school's reading prize. He drew up a list, watched over her progress, firmly kept her at her reading, and as she finished each book he quizzed her at length. Seager's tutoring was productive. His uncompromising, tough questions and his thorough discussions prepared Jane well for the nuns' questions. They were particularly amazed that such a young girl had so thoroughly comprehended the difficult and "racy" *Madame Bovary*. Jane did indeed become the first freshman to win the reading prize.

Nourished by loneliness, an isolation that had its roots in stubborn defiance and that continued to flower from a romantic attitude, the chief pursuits of Seager's life—learning, writing, and teaching—gained momentum during the Memphis years. In early 1924 his isolation became less artificial and less romantic. Emma Seager became a semi-invalid, gradually incapacitated by cancer. The disruption of the home, as described in Seager's notebooks, evokes the decline of Joyce's Dedalus household. Seager's sister declares that things were by no means that bad; however, the notebook must be an accurate reflection of Seager's emotional state. His grandfather Beauman Seager's favorite axiom, from Job, "Man is born for trouble as the sparks fly upward" had proved true again.[3] It would become a guiding principle.

Emma Seager's strong spirit as death approached impressed her son deeply, and it is easy enough to understand how he came to value stoical acceptance so highly and to conclude years later, as he examined his country, that an excess of hope underlay its many ills. Hope destroyed left only despair; the solution was obviously to forget hope and to accept the present, to temper the excessive native optimism. Emma Seager masked her great pain stoically in the presence of her children. The last time Seager saw his mother alive he was leaving her room when she called to him. As he turned to see what she wanted, she only smiled and winked. Before the day ended she was dead. Little wonder fortitude, strength, and acceptance in the face of adversity became virtues in Seager's eyes; little wonder both he and the protagonists of his novels exemplify these virtues.

Michigan and Oxford: Flight and Return

Seager eventually adapted very well to Memphis, but the Michigan of his childhood was still home, for as he emphasized again and again in his work, first definitions are never supplanted. His resolve to return home had remained firm, and on April 20, 1925, he took his application for admittance to the University of Michigan with him to high school to obtain the necessary signatures and official records. The day's journal entry reflects an attitude toward American education that remained virtually unchanged throughout his life: "The entrance requirements are so low that I wonder their halls are not filled with chattering morons. They probably are."[4] In September he returned to Michigan to enter the university, and he soon concluded that his prejudgment had been essentially correct. Seager's feeling of intellectual superiority was genuine; it is an example of the unflinching honesty that (without the youthful priggishness, to be sure) was so often mistaken in his later life for arrogance.

The differences between Seager and the average student—and, indeed, as he soon discovered, the average professor—was that for him knowledge was as much an end as a means. Others hoped to use a degree to acquire good jobs, security, or status. For Seager the degree was secondary—as his failure to pay the fee entitling him to the M.A. from Oxford until 1947, thirteen years after he qualified for it, attests. The value of knowledge was, for him, a given; facts, details, information are packed into his fiction, making it a potential gold mine for future social historians.

At Michigan Seager gradually acquired an ingredient essential to his development as a writer, empathy. Examining his own intellectual superiority, he discovered not so much the reasons for his own brilliance as for the general lack of it among American students. He concluded that intellectual superiority was not considered an asset for a number of reasons, especially that it set one off from the crowd. This discovery suggested that perhaps he "kept [his] sensitivity pumped up too high," and that his scorn resulted from the tensions of this pumping.[5]

Seager continued to observe, but he began to temper his scorn, to lower the tensions of his own sensitivity; he attempted to understand rather than to condemn. The change is obviously paralleled by the one Charles Berry makes in *Amos Berry*. As with Charles and Amos Berry, the need to understand became almost an obsession with Allan Seager. An excellent description of Seager's years at Michigan is to be found in his biography of Theodore Roethke, *The Glass House*. Roethke and Seager were contemporaries at Michigan; and, though Charles Berry is primarily Allan Seager, undergraduate, a reader of *The Glass House* will catch glimpses of Theodore Roethke in the fictional poet, Charles Berry.

Seager's career at Michigan was notable both academically and socially. As a star swimmer, he was literally pulled to the center of campus social life. He soon pledged a "top" fraternity, Psi Upsilon, although it had to accept him on his own terms. He refused to submit to hazing. Such refusal to accede to strong pressure from the group when he felt it was either wrong or absurd often manifested itself, but shrewd judgment no doubt underlay it, for rarely did such refusals result in his ostracism. Seager's notebook shows amusement at individuals passionately pledging to serve an impersonal organization created to serve them; only later would he find the implications of such behavior sinister. For the time being he could reconcile his own strong individualism with his scorn for "joiners" by assuring himself that he was merely an outsider on the inside, a spy of sorts who always kept one cold eye scanning the walls for cracks.

Seager's tenure at Michigan was marred by one interruption. At the end of his first semester the arrangements that had been made for Jane in

Memphis broke down, and he returned to take care of her. The return to Memphis was painful, but his sense of familial loyalty and his self-discipline wouldn't let him do otherwise. To deny himself Michigan, especially with the glory and success coming to him, was a noble gesture. The poet Donald Hall intends a touch of irony when he calls this streak in Seager "nobility." Hall feels that Seager often "nobly" imposed unnecessary restrictions upon himself when, if he had asked, others would gladly have helped him. But Seager invariably kept his troubles to himself, practicing a species of self-reliance that later seemed to border on masochism. Dignity was an important word for Seager, and stoicism, a quiet acceptance of misfortune while presenting an inscrutable expression to the world, was central to his definition. Yet in his fiction, while self-reliance is a virtue, it is shown to have a dark side. None of his characters achieves complete self-reliance, and those who attempt it invariably suffer—most notably Amos Berry and Hugh Canning.

The hiatus in Memphis produced one benefit, the under-the-counter purchase on May 13, 1926, of a second edition of James Joyce's *Ulysses*, one of only a handful of copies in the United States at the time. The agonizing decision to invest the enormous sum of fifty dollars in a book, especially for a young man saving his money to return to college, is an indication of his priorities. Literature was of singular importance. Seager's literary tastes were, to say the least, advanced. When he returned to Michigan, Seager wrote a paper for class, "The Scheme of *Ulysses*," which was certainly as good as any guides that had been published up to that time. It is an indication of his literary abilities that as a college sophomore Seager understood *Ulysses* better than most contemporary critics and scholars.[6]

Seager returned to Michigan in the fall of 1926, having placed Jane with relatives in Adrian. He maintained both his disciplined approach to learning and his status as an "insider" by studying a consistent six hours on the sly during the day. Thus he was able to be openly social in the evenings, drinking, partying, and wooing with the best of them. Studying was like drinking: it afforded the dual pleasure of simultaneous rebellion and conformity. He gave the appearance of belonging, and he did belong, but at the same time he followed his own dictates. He studied individuals functioning in groups; he learned not only from classes and reading but from observation.

While swimming was a means at Michigan, bringing him glory, women, and social acceptance, it was also an end. He swam because he enjoyed it. Because Michigan was a national power, swimming brought an unexpected bonus, the opportunity to visit most of the major cities in the country. While he didn't shun partying and horseplay with his teammates, Seager did manage to slip off for personal tours of each city. In Philadelphia for national qualifications, for example, he took an historical tour of the city. His visit to Independence Hall found its way, nearly thirty years later, into *Amos Berry*, and the question he asked himself as he viewed the "portraits of the early conscript fathers by Charles Wilson Peale" is in a vein similar to the questions his fiction so desperately seeks to answer: "What do these proper gentlemen think of the Mammon they began?"[7]

He took advantage of the trips to broaden his experience in many ways, passing up team meals so that he could visit restaurants of some reputation "in order to increase [his] all too meagre knowledge of gastronomy." He always observed: on one train trip to Chicago he struck up a conversation with a German-speaking couple from Schleswig-Holstein, using his own German to quiz them, as well as he was able, about their homeland and their reactions to the United States.

In Seager's fiction people are always "breaking out." Company executives abandon their careers to become farmers. Husbands who are apparently married automata suddenly risk scandal to seek mistresses. A bank teller absconds with cash the day of his retirement in order to fly to Paris and take a lover. The son of a proper businessman refuses to work and escorts a local prostitute to a country club party. Of all those who attempt to break out, few are successful, but those who are trapped and fail to make any escape attempt are the living dead.

Seager himself longed to break out, to make a getaway not just from the provincial morality of the Midwest, but from the United States itself. He contemplated a Rhodes Scholarship as early as 1926, and he knew his chances were good: he was an all-American swimmer, he was Phi Beta Kappa, and he had the *savoir-faire* most of his contemporaries lacked. Seager became a Rhodes Scholar, and he was thus able to break away in style. In October, 1930, at the age of twenty-four, he entered Oriel College, Oxford.

That England had a great effect on him is indisputable. From England he was able to see America with greater objectivity than ever before, and thus he made the remarkable discovery that recurs in his fiction: it is virtually impossible to escape one's roots. If peace is to be found, it is essential first to come to terms with one's heritage. The difference between "this town" and Salamanca may be very great indeed, but even in fleeing to Salamanca, "this town" is never left behind.

Seager's immediate impression, and one that was generally true, was that he had escaped to sympathetic soil. He admired that quality in the

British that enabled them to mask joy and despair with the same nonchalant expression and to perform the most heroic deeds coolly, almost offhandedly. After observing the British manner, and especially the Oxford manner, he found Dunkirk not the least bit surprising a few years later. Adopting the "Oxford manner" proved simple for Seager; the Seager manner had been similar for years.

At Oxford he studied openly rather than in secret, and it was immediately apparent that his colleagues would understand if at any time he chose study over social life. His actual routine changed little, except for long conversations on "serious" subjects. He spent "about five hours a day at books," attended a "couple of lectures," rowed for two hours (substituting one grueling water sport for another), socialized, and kept journal notes. As he began to look at England more objectively, he noticed that despite the trappings afforded by a thousand extra years of history, disagreeable similarities between America and "the empire" existed. He wrote his father ridiculing a speech by a Governor of Uganda, "simply an educated Rotarian" who spoke of "raising the average of civilization," but meant only to "educate the world to drink tea and drive Ford cars."[8]

Seager's feelings for England didn't diminish; he simply recovered his realist's slant after the initial enthusiasm at "escaping." While his fellow students were intellectually capable, they were, Seager discovered, in many ways as childish and immature as American students. Of more import was the realization that they viewed education in much the same manner as their American counterparts: a requirement for bettering oneself, a means to security, a good job, an appointment to a lucrative post. The attitude was less obvious in England—pleasantly masked, but present. The resumption of his realist's outlook brought with it the suspicion that one doesn't escape one's heritage by leaving it, a lesson a number of Seager's protagonists learn. Clearly, England's history was not his history, and although his maternal grandfather was English-born, Seager was still in a foreign country.

Seager began as brilliantly at Oxford as he had at Michigan. His tutor, Percy Simpson, expected Seager to be his first student in many years to take a First in examinations. Seager rowed for Oriel, and he swam for Oxford, winning a "half-blue," a remarkable achievement for an American at that time. In addition to studies and sports, Seager continued to "broaden his experiences" by traveling to the Continent, especially Paris, whenever vacations permitted.

However, Beauman Seager's favorite dictum, "Man is born for trouble as the sparks fly upward," was brought home to him once again. Late in

February, 1932, Seager began to feel lethargic and to keep more and more to his room. His "slight indisposition" was soon diagnosed as tuberculosis, and his stay at Oxford halted abruptly. Seager departed in the true Oxford syle, remarkings "Six month, from now I'll either be cured or dead."[9] He returned to the United States for rest and treatment at Trudeau Sanitarium at Saranac Lake, New York, where he would stay for nearly a year.

During a brief layover at the University of Michigan's hospital, Seager's sister visited him. He rose from his bed and announced, " Well, it may kill me, but I'm not going without dancing with you one more time." He wound up the record player and danced around the room with her until she made him quit, afraid that he might indeed do himself harm. The incident is characteristic of the manner in which Seager faced the disease. He accepted it and went on living as best he could. As mentioned, the ability to accept adversity is central to his fiction.

Seager's recovery is described in "The Cure." Trudeau was pivotal, and Seager recognized it as such. It provided him with the material for some of his best work: "Pro Arte," "The Last Return," and the hospital scenes in *The Inheritance*. But more important, it provided the push he needed. After Trudeau, things fell quickly into place. There can be no doubt: tuberculosis decided Seager's career. He often gives characters in his fiction a similar jolt to disrupt the habits their lives have become.

Writer and Teacher

University officials marvelled that he returned at all, but in the spring of 1933 Seager went back to Oxford and earned a Second on his examinations. Tuberculosis probably robbed him of a First; and, though he expected a recurrence of the disease for the rest of his life, the illness had its benefits. Seager said often that while he had long wanted to be a writer, it was only the sense of his own mortality that gave him the needed impetus to begin writing.

Immediately after taking and passing "Schools," Seager successfully applied to the Rhodes Foundation for a third year of study. With resumption of his studies four months away and no money to indulge his usual vacation pastime, travel, he suddenly had time on his hands. Time and his sense of mortality were the necessary ingredients; the product was his first published short story.

Seager stayed at a pub, The Rose Revived, in East Hanney, Berkshire, because it was cheap. The Rhodes Foundation had alloted him thirty-eight pounds for the four months. He had few distractions, and he worked hard trying to write "one story as good as one of Maupassant's." He wrote sixty pages, boiled them down to six, and then began revising. "It was the first time I had ground anything down so I couldn't say it any other way," Seager wrote.[10] He was sick of the story by the time he finished it, but felt he had done his best. The story, "The Street," was published in the *London Mercury*; and measured solely on its staying power, it was an uncommon first story.

"The Street" has been published in "revised" form with amazing regularity. It has appeared in American magazines, British magazines, twice on British radio, and at least twice on American television. Each time it has been offered as an "original." Seager himself ran across the story in Portuguese when, in Brazil, he picked up a magazine to pass the time in a doctor's waiting room—again it was "written" by someone else. Seager was inclined to believe that the story had become an oral tale; in fact, a student in one of his own creative writing classes gave him a variation of "The Street" as an example of an oral tale suitable for conversion into a short story. Seager's first story was a special triumph, even if the recurring plagiarism aggravated him, for he had matched the master, his father, in the art of storytelling.

Seager discovered his *métier* writing "The Street" in East Hanney, and he was determined that nothing would keep him from it any longer, not even Oxford. When he returned to Oriel, he immediately changed tutors, from Percy Simpson to Edmund Blunden, because Blunden was an active poet and writer and understood the new focus of Seager's "studies." Seager wrote his father as the semester began: "I am supposed to be studying 19th C. literature, but I am really writing and getting his [Blunden's] criticism." He later wrote his father again, telling him that about the only thing he studied was "short stories—seeing how they're put together, and Christ I love it. It's just what I've been groping for in the last ten years."[11]

A friend showed some of Seager's work to E. J. O'Brien, editor of the annual *Best Short Stories*, and the immediate result was a meeting between the two. The meeting led to the writing of "This Town and Salamanca," one of the classic American short stories; O'Brien included it in his 1935 "Best" annual. Seager continued to write at Oxford, and he continued to see O'Brien, who encouraged him. As his final Oxford term neared its end, he began to consider employment. When he was offered a job with Jonathan Cape by Rupert Hart Davis, he politely declined, realizing that the place for a serious American writer was America. He resolved to return, despite the Great Depression, even if he had to deliver telegrams.

He landed in New York City in June, 1934, with three letters of introduction from E. J. O'Brien: to Whit Burnett, to Manuel Komroff, and to Charles Angoff. It didn't take long for the combined efforts of O'Brien, Komroff, and Burnett to persuade Frank Crowninshield and Condé Nast, editors of *Vanity Fair*, to hire a new assistant editor. Seager was pleased to be working at *Vanity Fair*. Though he was casual about it with friends, his notes reveal that he thoroughly enjoyed the prestige.

Vanity Fair provided a concentrated apprenticeship. Seager was forced to write short stories against a deadline. He wrote thirteen stories for *Vanity Fair* in a year and a half. In addition to his writing, he performed editorial duties as well, including shepherding subjects for *Vanity Fair*'s famous photographic essays to one of the masters: Edward Steichen, Lusha Nelson, or Margaret Bourke-White.

The job afforded Seager the opportunity to meet a virtual Who's Who of the middle 1930s: Joe Louis, H. G. Wells, Sean O'Casey, Ann Sothern, Katharine Hepburn, Huey Long, Roy Howard, Henrik Van Loon, William Saroyan, Walt Disney, Luigi Pirandello, Paul Gallico, Gary Cooper, Earl Carroll, Cole Porter, Moss Hart, Loretta Young, and even Dorothy Cleary, who was then supposed to be the "American woman Dickens." This is only a fraction of the great and near-great with whom Seager mingled, and he was surprised at his own casual attitude— he had no need to employ his Oxford manner for he was unawed. He wrote Edmund Blunden of life among the elite: "I meet such weltbe-kannte figures as Huey Long and Katharine Hepburn (who to my shock is slightly bandy-legged) but they have all left me unimpressed, Blasé— I'm getting."[12]

New York was a welcome opportunity for one who liked to get "the inside dope" and who loved to observe people, both nearly to the point of obsession. But the glittering surface of New York distracted Seager from the "real" writing he wanted to move on to. *Vanity Fair* was nearing its end, and Seager felt he was too "heavy" and thought too "slowly" for the light and flashy stuff empty-headed society people required. Neither the prestige nor the paycheck could keep him content, so that by the spring of 1935 he had decided to return to Michigan. Through quiet and careful inquiry he learned that the University of Michigan would be willing to hire him as an Instructor; and, Thomas Wolfe's declaration to the contrary, home was the place to go, a lesson his own fiction taught again and again, for one had to accept and understand one's roots before it was possible to gain solid control of one's life.

Seager's return to Ann Arbor in the fall of 1935 at the age of twenty-nine initiated an association that, with a few brief interruptions, lasted to the end of his life. New York had provided him with yet another angle of vision, with lodes of information, with the opportunity to hone his craft, with "contacts." It also provided one final gift—a Wrigley gum executive, impressed with Seager's reputation as a short story writer, made him the amazing offer of over two hundred dollars a week to script the *Scattergood Baines* radio show. Seager declined on the grounds that he was leaving for Michigan, but the executive persisted. Seager was allowed to mail in the scripts, on the condition that he travel to Chicago every two weeks to discuss the show. He was granted a co-scripter, author George Milburn, and together they turned out about three years' worth of scripts. Writing dialogue —even for lightweight entertainment—tuned Seager's ear even more finely than it was at the time.

The radio money enabled him to buy a farm in Onsted and set his father up as a farmer. But Seager remained in Ann Arbor for three more years. Hugh Kenner put into words what many people wondered: "And what was he doing, the unspoken question ran, professing at a midwestern university after Oriel College and *Vanity Fair*, this town and Salamanca?"[13]

The question is a fair one, and one that only his life and his fiction can answer. It is clear that Seager was home: "It is funny how much the weather means when you can see it instead of just feeling it. The equinoctial storms have just got to town, and they are pretty fine, and I can hear trees blowing at night."[14] And "I was over home [Adrian] the other day. The country cries out for someone like Breughel to do it but in upstairs sitting rooms old ladies still paint china."[15] This area became the setting for Seager's last four novels. And these people he had grown up hating now interested him above all others. He would be their Breughel.

Seager quickly decided that he would not waste time working on a Ph.D. The courses were too easy, and the professors could teach him little about literature. "I have heard all they say, so I don't take notes, which the other students think is snotty, and they are right. Now that I see my former instructors as colleagues, I think they are stupid almost to a man. . . . Of literature as a living thing, they seem to have no information, and nobody is likely to tell them about it, and so their talk about it smells of the tomb."[16]

Academia fares poorly in Seager's fiction. In *Amos Berry*, Ph.D. work is evidence of the intellectual death accompanying specialization. A number of Seager's short stories treat "scholars" harshly. If he had such contempt for academe, why did he stay? One reason was the strong sense of personal responsibility which informs his fiction. He remained in teaching to the end of his life because he wanted to make a difference, and as the unnamed poet says in "The Great Turtle Migration," "It's got to be an inside job." In addition, he loved learning; at Michigan he was close to a great library. Finally, he respected genuinely serious teachers and scholars; he learned from them, too.

He became, as James Michener noted in a 1950 *Saturday Review* article, one of the great American teachers. He was, as writer Josh Greenfeld observes, "a hell of a man to encounter at a pivotal time."[17] Seager's instruction transcended classroom walls. Certainly he meant his books to teach; he meant them to reach the average reader. For years he drove to Adrian once a week to lead a Great Books discussion group, and in both Onsted and Tecumseh he had long discussions with people— young or old—who were interested or interesting. He talked for hours about the Constitution and American history with James Goodrich, his model for the protagonist of *Hilda Manning*, and when Goodrich showed an interest in poetry, Seager encouraged him to read it and to write it.

Educating people, learning from people, these things were essential to Seager's life. He wanted people aware of the extent to which their lives were controlled by outside forces—movies, television, advertising, history, family. One of the lessons of *Amos Berry*, and a frequent theme in Seager's fiction, is that one must unlearn one's automatic responses in order to be free.

Seager's teaching was interrupted briefly on occasion. In the summer and fall of 1937 he and George Milburn traveled first to Chicago, then to Hollywood to get more closely involved with the production of the *Scattergood Baines* radio show. The company had been very impressed with the Milburn-Seager scripts; the show was carried on nine stations when their scripts began running, and within a year it was carried nationally, with ratings that delighted the Wrigley executives. The executives hoped Seager and Milburn would work more of their magic in Hollywood, and though the duo had only a vague notion of what they were to do—other than continue writing scripts and observe production of the show—they accepted the mission, primarily as a vacation.

While Seager later confirmed the reality of *The Day of the Locust* by Milburn's friend "Pep" West, he never attacked the Californians as bitterly as he had his own Michigan neighbors. In fact, he worried that people grew soft in lotus-land without storms to brace them. Once again he had gained an extra-environmental perspective. He puzzled over the reasons why he had little but anger for the people he grew up among but easily empathized with these Californian strangers. He began to comprehend that the heart of his discontent with his Michigan neighbors was not hatred for them, but hatred for whatever it was that kept them from realizing their capabilities.

In the summer of 1939 Seager accompanied Milburn to his home in Pineville, Missouri, to collaborate on a script stockpile. Because of the stifling heat, the two wrote in a cave, but the discomfort had its rewards. The trip provided Seager with the material for a number of short stories, including "The Old Man of the Mountain." He also returned from Pineville with yet another perspective on Michiganders and on the changing quality of life in America. The people of the Ozarks seemed as yet untouched by the restraint under which most Northerners labored. They reacted with open affection, anger, even violence, with little concern for the opinions of others. The crucial difference, for Seager, was that these people were in more direct control of their lives than their counterparts in Michigan where industrialization was making life secondhand.

Secondhand in this way: a man's occupation was no longer directly related to his survival. A Michigan dairy farmer who produced hundreds of times more milk than he himself could consume and—worse—never saw his consumers and a man bolting on a single part in an automobile assembly line had something in common: the abstraction of immediate meaning from their work. The experiences of Hollywood and Pineville crystallized the notions that had been working in Seager's mind. He was ready to present the whole view; he was ready at last to write novels.

Novelist and Prophet

Two important changes took place in Seager's life when he returned to Michigan in the autumn of 1939. Because his father had suffered a stroke and could no longer manage the farm alone, Seager moved to Onsted to help him. And after teaching, writing for radio, and five "clean" years without tuberculosis, he finally felt secure enough to marry. On November 10, 1939, he married Barbara Watson.

The farm proved an ideal place to write, and at first it was an idyllic environment for a newly married couple. But the usual Seager misfortune plagued it. Arch Seager never fully recovered from his stroke. Then when World War II broke out, the hired hand who compensated for Arch's disability was drafted. A series of minor misfortunes arrived like the plagues on Egypt. The fate of the turkey flock was typical. At the outset of the war an air strip near Onsted was used to train pilots, and since the Seager farm had the only white barn in the area, someone decided it would make a fine target for mock air raids. The first raid had real casualties. When one turkey, hearing the approaching roar, raised his head first in question and then in panic, ran headlong into the side of the barn and broke his neck, the others followed. They battered their heads against the barn until the flock was decimated. Though Seager loved to tell the story and laugh a few years later, it was a cruel blow for a farm making, at best, a marginal profit.

The success of the farm was artistic, not agricultural; it was prime source material for his fiction. The farm served as background for two novels, *Amos Berry* and *Hilda Manning*. Seager's Onsted neighbors walk their pages, and the novels are well served by the farming knowledge Seager gained. He also enjoyed being where he could really feel the weather; he was convinced that here he could discern the effects of weather and land upon its inhabitants.

Seager kept plugging away at *the* novel. He wrote slowly, as he always wrote, and with care. Meanwhile he continued teaching, farming, and corresponding with friends who had been drafted. A striking feature of the Bancroft Library's Allan Seager Collection is the vast number of letters to and from servicemen. It is another measure of his sense of responsibility. He had tried to enlist in the Navy after the Army rejected him—due to the lung deflated when he had tuberculosis. But the Navy also rejected him, and he attempted, with the aid of a local Congressman, to inviegle work in either Intelligence or the State Department but without success.

His desire to serve was only partially due to his sense of responsibility; he was driven as well by his desire to know, to get the "real lowdown" on the war. The letters were the next best way to get firsthand information. Forced to stay home, he finished the novel.

Equinox was published in 1943, and it was an immediate best seller. Movie rights were sold, and the novel was a Literary Guild selection. But a wartime paper shortage scotched the Literary Guild deal and abruptly halted *Equinox*'s sales at the forty thousand mark. In spite of the shortened press run, *Equinox* managed to create a stir; it is one more example of the Seager misfortune that it didn't gain the even wider circulation it was headed for—if it had, perhaps Seager would be better known today.

In 1943 his first child, Mary, was born. That same year he was promoted to Assistant Professor and given a substantial raise. But he was also approached by his friend Theodore Roethke with the suggestion that Seager join him at Bennington College. Seager applied, was accepted, and in the fall of 1944, having sold the Onsted farm, traveled to Vermont. Typically, Seager gained a new awareness of his environment by leaving it. Vermont gave him an insight into the relationship between men and land which he would explore in his next four novels. Once again he would return to Michigan with a fresh outlook, a slightly altered perspective.

The immediate response to the Vermont landscape was personal, and it was closely related to his developing thoughts on pioneerism. "I can understand my grandfather better now," he wrote in his journal. In New England his grandfather had struggled hard to gain a living from the land, clearing stones even before he could plant. "This expectation that life was going to be a narrow squeak he brought with him to Michigan where land was flat and life easier." Thus in Michigan what seemed "mean and close-handed" was simply the approach to life in Vermont which had been necessary to Beauman's survival. Behavior, which meant survival in Beauman's youth, had crystallized into habit.[18]

Seager gained new insight into the relationship between men and the land they worked. He discovered how the land had formed his grandfather's character and his attitudes, attitudes that he could not change when he changed his environment. Seager extended the principle. He applied it, in his fiction, not only to his family and to his own corner of Michigan, but also to the nation as a whole. Pioneer energy and spirit were increasingly smothered or twisted by the demands of the twentieth century.

At Bennington Seager observed Theodore Roethke in action, and these observations were to form the foundation of his biography of Roethke, *The Glass House*. Bennington was satisfying, yet Seager stayed for only one academic year. He enjoyed Vermont, but Michigan was home. He couldn't sever the ties, and he knew it; the need to return home was stronger than ever now that he had reached an even profounder understanding of the people among whom he had grown up.

Seager purchased a Victorian house with twelve-foot ceilings and Italian marble fireplaces in Tecumseh, twenty-six miles from Ann Arbor and ten minutes from both his boyhood home in Adrian and the farm in Onsted. He lived in that house the rest of his life. Soon after his return to Michigan he began working in earnest on *The Inheritance*. He was confident about the book, feeling none of the pressure he had experienced as he tried to write *Equinox*. Having been through the process once, he knew that he was a novelist, that he would write the book whatever the distractions. Soon the distractions were very grave indeed.

In 1948, the year Seager's second daughter, Laura, was born and the year he completed *The Inheritance*, his wife Barbara was discovered to have multiple sclerosis. Seager had already begun to view the novel as the proper medium for his serious art; consequently, he was writing stories primarily to support his novels. After Barbara's illness was diagnosed, he deliberately began to write slick fiction when he needed money for medical expenses. And since he read medical journals and took Barbara to specialists at any hint of a breakthrough in MS research, the use of orinase, for example, the expenses were considerable.

On February 10, 1949, Arch Seager died in Onsted. Though not unexpected, the death of his father, hard upon the knowledge of Barbara's illness, disheartened Seager. Yet his stoic attitude, his mask of aplomb, was misinterpreted by some as a lack of emotion. When his father died, Seager was writing *Amos Berry*, and the direction that novel took is an indication of his love for his father. It is one of the most sensitive treatments of a father-son relationship in American literature. Seager's reaction to adversity is revealed in a favorite line of his, one he gives to Charles Berry: "The place to exert your will is in the practice of the craft."

In 1950 a collection of Seager's previously published short stories was issued under the title *The Old Man of the Mountain*. Of the eighteen stories, eight had either been selected for various "Best Short Story" anthologies or won prizes, thus the generally good reviews were not surprising. Yet Seager was characteristically more concerned with current work than past work, and he had his highest hopes for *Amos Berry*.

When *Amos Berry* was published in 1953, it was well received by a few scattered individuals, who praised Seager as the "prophet come to lead America out of the wilderness," but few people read it. Seager's journal notes state simply, "I waited and I was disappointed. The book was not received well."[19] In his craft his will's choices had been made, and to his craft the will was irrevocably committed. There was nothing to do but try again.

Although worried by the Korean Police Action, harried by his wife's illness, in agony from lower back pains, and depressed by *Amos Berry*'s reception, Seager wrote furiously. His first three novels took almost exactly five years from early planning to finished manuscript. *Hilda Manning* took barely two. The intensity with which he wrote is an indication of the depth of his gloom. *Hilda Manning*, published in 1956, fared no better than *Amos Berry*. Seager considered these two books his best; he knew they were good. Yet they received much less attention than his earlier, less-polished novels. He was puzzled.

In the dark of his despair an idea had been glimmering. He would take a sabbatical leave from Michigan and get away to France, ostensibly to translate Stendahl's *Memoires d' un Touriste*, but in truth to try and recover some of the happiness France had bestowed upon him as a young man. The trip began well, and as the ship approached Le Havre, Seager was unable to sleep. He felt not excitement, but the "hope that France will do something for me. There should be no difference between the vitality and the spirit, but the one is high, the other low."[20]

Once again Seager had to learn the lesson he tried to teach in his fiction: one doesn't escape problems by avoiding them. The trip aborted after a few months. Seager gave the Suez crisis as the reason, but friends suspected Barbara's nerves, or Seager's nerves and Barbara's health. His final novel, *Death of Anger*, vividly and bitterly indicates the truth of the lesson that travel is not escape.

By 1959 Barbara could, on her best days, barely walk—and then only with help. On her worst days she was an invalid. But the opposed forces of passion and restraint that ruled Seager's life still governed. His despair was private. In class he never gave the slightest hint that he was troubled by anything other than ignorance and ineptitude. His mask never slipped.

Death of Anger appeared in 1960 with virtually no publicity because the publishing firm of McDowell-Obolensky was on the verge of failure when the novel was published. To the end of his life Seager bitterly referred to the novel as the book born in silence. It was indicative of the pattern of misfortune that plagued him that internal strife should doom the firm so soon after he had been persuaded to go with it.

Things got worse, and still he kept trying. He wrecked his car; his license was suspended. He had to depend on his daughter to drive him to Ann Arbor for classes. He planned for weeks ahead to get "roaring drunk" at the *Esquire* Writers Conference held at the University of Michigan October 27 and 28, 1961. Barbara was scheduled to enter St. Joseph's hospital for tests that weekend, and Seager looked forward to a brief relief from the strain of caring for her. The conference was a disaster.

A party at a professor's home, after the conference, turned mean, complete with smashed furniture and a lawsuit. And when Seager attempted to leave one last party at about three A.M., he fell down a steep flight of stairs and shattered his arm. "The median artery was thrown away, and the only clear evidence I have ever had of the value of my clean athletic life, the doc said, 'If you hadn't kept up the swimming the auxillary vessels wouldn't have taken over and you would have gotten gangrene and we would have had to cut the arm off at the elbow and put a hook on it.'"[21]

With most of the strength in his arm gone, Seager was forced at last to put Barbara in a nursing home. Even after the accident his sense of responsibility dictated that he try to take care of her at home, but when Laura's appendix burst, his options were ended. He simply couldn't do it alone. He continued to visit his wife regularly, often twice a day, fulfilling his "duty" as he saw it, but he couldn't help feeling his luck had changed. His spirits lifted, and events reinforced his feelings. His translation of Stendahl was, after twenty-one submissions, accepted for publication. The reviews were good, and the *New York Times* review appeared in the last issue before a newspaper strike.

Seager began work on a new novel, an hilarious account of his years with George Milburn working on the radio scripts. The protagonist is part George Milburn, part Allan Seager, and part Theodore Roethke— all the parts are eccentric artist. The novel was never finished; he suspended it to write a biography of Roethke.

The only work that vaguely resembles the unfinished novel is *A Frieze of Girls* (1964), which is consistently light-hearted, whimsically comic. *A Frieze of Girls* was a surprise best seller, and it points up an essential fact about Seager as an artist. He could be as witty and amusing in his fiction as he often was in conversation or in the classroom. He also understood the market; when he needed money he could write a slick "chugger" for almost automatic publication. Yet he avoided the temptation to write a chugging, best-selling novel. He hoped his books would sell well, that they would even be best sellers, but first and foremost he intended them to be serious books, to be part of an attempt to improve the quality of life in America.

By 1965 Seager was working in earnest on a biography of Roethke, his spirits still buoyed by the success of *A Frieze of Girls*. The Roethke research was so appealing that, for the first time in his life, he suspended work on a novel in progress. His enjoyment grew, no doubt, from the fact that Roethke's life was so much like his own. In fact, *The Glass House* is often as much about Allan Seager as about Theodore Roethke, as though through Roethke he could justify himself.

Barbara died during the writing of *The Glass House*, and as the book neared completion Seager began battling lung cancer. He was also battling Beatrice Roethke, Theodore Roethke's widow. Seager referred to the demands for cuts and revisions, the refusal to grant him permission to quote Roethke's poems in the book, as "Manchester problems." Hoping to see *The Glass House* in print before he died, Seager began to make concessions, agreeing to cuts he had refused previously. On May 10, 1968, Seager died of a coronary blood clot. On the day of his death only one of his books was still in print, *Death of Anger*, and it was in print only because of legal complications unresolved at McDowell-Obolensky's breakup.

Six months after Seager's death *The Glass House* was published. The English critic, John Davenport, called it a masterpiece and said that Seager was the best "non-academic critic writing in English."[22] Hugh Kenner declares that it "is simply the best American biography."[23] As good as it is, the original manuscript was better.

The Quality of His Life: A Triumph

The Glass House is brilliant, and its brilliance is an accurate measure of the odd chasm between the quality of Seager's work and his reputation. Seager's fiction was autobiographical, and so was his nonfiction. Even in writing the biography of another man, Seager wrote about himself. Ultimately his subject was always himself, and he knew it. Seager contended that an evaluation of an artist's work was invariably and inescapably an evaluation of his life. This belief was not in harmony with an era that had embraced the New Critics, and it is a belief that surely contributed to Seager's relative obscurity.

A sweeping survey of Seger's life is misleading, for it implies a life of promise met at every juncture by misfortune. Certainly Seager had more than his share of bad luck, but he persevered. He accepted it and kept trying, often triumphing over it—when necessity forced him to cook, he became superb at it, an artist. The attitude he displayed was the same one he made essential to the protagonists of his fiction, and just as the details of his fiction shouldn't be overlooked, the details of his life shouldn't be ignored. For here was his triumph.

Seager's primary concern was the quality of life, which he felt was being steadily diminished by powerful forces at work in the modern world. He worked and wrote in an attempt to improve the general quality of life, and it is very easy, attending to the large picture, to overlook the quality of his personal life—the eye-catching misfortune is partially to blame, of course.

According to Seager's second wife, Joan Seager Fry, one thing "that's absolutely imperative to understanding Allan is 'the quality of the life.'" "The quality of the life is champagne after dinner. Elegant meals. Long intense intelligent talks until 1:30 in the morning, beautiful sexual women, old jazz, faded wine-colored wing chairs, an original Whistler pen-and-ink on the wall, very unobtrusive, an original Daumier in the study, the gloom of a hundred-year-old house lit but only partially by golden firelight from an Italian marble fireplace. Add enough things together—real material things—and you will get it."[24]

Then add people to the things: the incipient juvenile delinquents he took under his arm, the innumerable students he aided, the amusing residents of Tecumseh who kept him entertained—the same people he hated as a young man—and for whom he felt a whimsical affection that bordered at times on love. The famous and not-so-famous artists, writers, and poets who trooped through Onsted and Tecumseh to visit him—from Sherwood Anderson and Carl Sandburg to Theodore Roethke and Thomas Kinsella. Seager never doubted that Old Beauman was right to quote Job, "Man is born for trouble as the sparks fly upward." But knowing that, and then accepting it, the quality of life between troubles could be made superb indeed.

Chapter Two
The Short Stories
Starting at the Top

Allan Seager began at the top as a short story writer. His very first story, "The Street," was published in the *London Mercury* in January, 1934. His second story, "This Town and Salamanca," was selected by E. J. O'Brien for inclusion in *The Best Short Stories of* 1935, and O'Brien dedicated that volume to Seager and William Saroyan. In a *World-Telegram* interview O'Brien named Seager third in the "apostolic succession of the American short story" behind only Sherwood Anderson and Ernest Hemingway. And in a WJZ radio interview O'Brien said that "This Town and Salamanca" was one of the four best stories, out of over 150,000, that he had ever read.[1] Beginning in the summer of 1934 Seager published fourteen stories in *Vanity Fair* in barely a year and a half. It is interesting to speculate, given this spectacular beginning, what he might have accomplished in the genre had he not been determined to become a novelist.

Seager's collection, *The Old Man of the Mountain* (1950), amply demonstrates his remarkable range in technique, milieu, and characterization. Stories are set in England, South America, Tennessee, and Michigan; milieus are urban and rural, academic and backwoods, lower class and aristocratic. Seven of the stories were either prize winners or selections for annual "best" anthologies.

His extraordinary first story, "The Street," many times rewritten by others, has no doubt succeeded in its plagiarized versions because of the plot's basic appeal. Two patients are confined to beds in a hospital. One patient is by the room's only window, and he describes in vivid detail the daily events on the tree-lined sunlit street outside. The other patient grows covetous of the window vantage point and, eventually, rather than call the night nurse when his roommate suffers an attack, he lets him die in order to inherit the bed by the window. Once moved, he discovers that the street and its inhabitants were fictitious; the window looks out on a blank courtyard which is empty all day.

Seager's version surpasses the imitations because it goes well beyond the mere coveting of an imaginary view, whereas his imitators rely on plot, especially the surprise ending, completely. Seager's unnamed protagonist gradually considers himself engaged in a quest for the window and believes that to prove himself worthy he must defeat Death Himself. Death is his roommate Whitaker, who soon becomes simply "He." Thus this simple story assumes archetypal overtones.

Seager never strays far from the realistic surface. As the protagonist's disease progresses, he feels less remorse for his anger at Whitaker, who "held one end of the thread that led back into what he was coming to call 'life.'"[2] At sundown, when his fever increases and the "daytime clarity" of his mind vanishes, he begins to have the fantasy that Whitaker is Death guarding "the gateway to life." His illness causes his fantasy to become conviction, just as Whitaker's causes him to indeed resemble Death as he grows more gaunt.

Seager was ever careful to provide a realistic framework for archetypal elements. Myth, symbol, psychology, sociology, the elements never obstructed the progress of the basic story. A master craftsman, he blended elements smoothly, so smoothly that most critics and reviewers failed to get beyond the surface of his works. In "The Street," for example, he employs the venerable symbolism of seasons, but manages it so subtly that it is unobtrusive.

The evolution of the protagonist's fantasy is paralleled by the progress of the seasons. The story opens in spring, and anger and fever grow all through the "empty summer" until he resolves to let Whitaker die. With the advent of autumn, the fantasy that Whitaker is Death becomes, for the protagonist, reality. And aware that "winter's coming," the windowless protagonist no longer desires Whitaker's bed simply to view the street; he wants "to bring back the year," to defeat Death, who "wants the year to die, also" (5).

The protagonist plans to "make this bleak season blossom as the rose" once he overthrows Whitaker-Death. He will be a beneficent ruler in the mad tyrant's place. Seager's story has a double irony; the blank, empty courtyard is the obvious irony on which the plot hinges. Yet once the protagonist is moved into Whitaker's bed, he will certainly have the power to make the kingdom pleasant, to bring back the year, for it must be a kingdom of his imagination as it was for Whitaker.

The seasonal parallel, with its suggestion of the birth-death-rebirth cycle, functions on two levels. On the night Whitaker dies, rain spatters on the window, and Whitaker, as he is dying, breaks into "long dry sobs." Thus both the dry and the wet, death and rebirth, accompany his death. The Fisher King motif is obvious. Moved into the bed by the window, the protagonist carefully arranges his pillows, "making ready to look out as one who had come into a kingdom" (6,7). The king is dead, long live the king.

The fable—and certainly this story has the lasting elements of the best fables—illustrates a lesson Seager's fiction teaches again and again. No man who relies entirely upon the imagination of others can be happy. With William Blake and George Bernard Shaw, Seager believed that imagination was the first step in creating the real world, and he felt that one cause of the growing unhappiness in twentieth-century America was that modern Americans were trying to bring to life the dreams of their pioneer forebears. Rather than engaging the imagination in the creation of a dream to fit their own world, Americans had simply assumed dream and imagination from their predecessors.

Later Seager wrote that Americans needed "to instal death in the dream so that, knowing the term, life can mean something. The American dream was all right (Not good, but all right) as long as the future was a place to go."[3] For "The Street"'s protagatonist, the future was the bed by the window. Once he reaches the physical limits of this frontier, his dream is dead because it was another's dream. His imagination has worked only to destroy that dream; it has been self-defeating. Thus no kingdom is possible but the one he must fashion from his own imagination, the dream that must come from within.

This is merely one implication of the story, but it is an idea that Seager presented repeatedly in his fiction. He postulated later that the quality of modern life was poor because the will was nearly paralyzed, and this paralysis was, in part, a failure of the imagination.

Like the best fables, "The Street" rewards contemplation with meaning. The story can be read as a parable that illustrates the artist's usual fate. Destruction threatens those who do shape reality with their imaginations. Seager's fiction shows that it is a risky business. Witness his novel *Amos Berry*.

"The Street" is solid evidence that Seager could carefully consider his audience. It was first published in England, where Seager submitted it under the name J. B. A. Seager because he felt the editor was more likely to take him for an Englishman. The minor revisions he made when the story was collected in *The Old Man of the Mountain* indicate his subtlety. The English "garden" becomes "backyard" in the American version, and "motor" becomes "car." The protagonist's "walking tour of Brittany" becomes "his winter in Mexico." The typist has a "bouquet" rather than a "posy," and while Whitaker originally "gave" his sobs, in the U.S. version he "broke into" them. "Pity you didn't hear poor Whitaker" was fine for an English doctor, but an American doctor must say "Too bad you didn't hear poor Whitaker last night." And in the English version the courtyard was "quite empty," whereas in the American it is merely "empty."

Seager made nearly three dozen revisions, all of them minor—most of them substitutions of Americanisms for Anglicisms. It would have been easy enough to let a sixteen-year-old story stand as it had been published twice before, but Seager was a meticulous writer and a man who cared about his craft. This first story is typical of his central concern with the necessity of creating one's own dream rather than relying on the dreams of others. And it is evidence of his craftsmanship.

His second story, "This Town and Salamanca," more than fulfills the promise of his first. It may be his best story; it is certainly his best-known and most widely anthologized. Seager sold it almost immediately after its completion: it appeared in the May, 1934, issue of *Life and Letters*. *Story* then bought it at the suggestion of E. J. O'Brien and printed it in August. It has been reprinted a number of times since.

In "This Town and Salamanca" friends of John Baldwin eagerly hang upon the tales of his travels. They encourage him to tell the tales each time he returns home, and they make them the basis of their own dreams. Through John Baldwin the others escape "this town," and through him they manage to cling to the promises youth once held. However, when John Baldwin returns to "this town" to settle down, begins to develop a paunch, abandons fencing for golf, and becomes a banker, their dreams are shattered, their youth is lost. The final words of the story, "But our youth only" (92) make the conflict between doers and dreamers explicit. The emphasis falls unmistakably upon the "our." John Baldwin has not lost his youth; he has lived it.

The obvious parallel between "The Street" and "This Town and Salamanca" is that in both stories the product of one man's imagination becomes the dream of reality for another. In both stories the tapestry the dream weaver has woven is revealed as his exclusive property. The conflict between "this town" and Salamanca is a clash often reenacted in Seager's fiction.

"This Town and Salamanca" begins abruptly, and the opening paragraph relies heavily upon pronouns: "So when he returned, we asked him why he had gone to live there and he said he'd just heard of it and thought it might be a nice place to live in for a while" (80). As in "The Street," the use of pronouns suggests interchangeable antecedents for "he," "we," "it," and "this town," thereby implying the universality of the situation: "this town" could be any midwestern American town. John Baldwin courteously keeps himself out of his stories ("John was seldom an actor in his own play—he merely looked, it seemed, and told us what he saw. It was the best way, keeping himself out. . . ." [82, 83]) so the listeners can easily slip onto the stage of their dreams.

The reader knows almost from the beginning that John Baldwin has returned to "this town" to settle down, yet the lyrical unraveling of the wanderer's exploits, the revelation of the symbiotic relationship between the wanderer's wandering and the dreamers' dreams, leaves the reader prey to an irony as powerful as the ending of "The Street," but without that story's O. Henry twist. Had John Baldwin simply returned, the irony would be simple and obvious, but Baldwin returns and finds his happiness in becoming exactly like those who have so envied him. When his friends attempt to get him to talk about past adventures, he returns to banking matters, to the mundane question of a loan for a local farmer. Asked if he still fences, Baldwin attempts lunges and parries with a golf club, the recreational tool of the cliché businessman, and laughingly comments that he is getting fat and can't do them anymore.

Details are the life of this story: the description of the *braseros* and slanting sills of Salamanca, the observation that in Salamanca "the cathedral had small windows and the light was yellow inside, not like the gray light inside the cathedrals in the Ile de France," the "bigger and bigger stitches in the canvas" as Baldwin realized sharks would quickly undo the shrouds he was sewing, all of these exemplify the Seager method.

Hugh Kenner speaks of the Seager "knowingness" as very like Hemingway's, except that "Hemingway's is a tone; the Seager method extends into minute crevices of fact."[4] In "This Town and Salamanca," facts and tangible "things" are artfully presented and contrasted to reinforce the story's theme. The golf club is the exact "thing" to contrast with a foil. The narrator's own lost dreams are made concrete in the gold moidore John Baldwin acquired in Port-au-Prince. The boat Baldwin builds, shaving teak with its "acrid leather odor" for its deck, is at the heart of the contrast between John Baldwin and his friends, between "this town" and Salamanca: "The things we saw every day, the houses, trees, and grain elevators, went straight up from the ground. They had roots. . . . John's boat was a strange shape, curved for the water" (84, 85). The narrator realizes that "The boat had sprung from some matrix in him that we would never understand" (85).

The difference between this midwestern town and the exotic places John Baldwin has visited is primarily a catalog of "things." When Baldwin returned to see his mother, "he would tell us these things that made us seem fools to ourselves for having stayed," but Baldwin settles for what they had remained and worked for: "the same trees every day when you go to work, in summer handing over the lawns beside the walks, and bare with snow at the forks of the limbs and the sound of snow shovels scraping the walks; and when you look up, the line of the roof of the house next door against the sky. You could call it peace. It is just peace with no brilliance. I remember how bright the gold piece was in his hand" (90).

Seager manipulates "things" so brilliantly in the story, that when John Baldwin is misled by "things" of "this town" (a big combine, a radio, a Packard) into making a bad loan, the reader feels empathy not for Baldwin, but for the narrator, for in becoming aware of Baldwin's misreading of the value of "things," the narrator has arrived at the stunning insight into his own self-deception.

The story is artfully constructed. Its inherent duality is suggested by the title, and it is reinforced in the form: sections one and three complement each other, as do sections two and four. The "tunnel of green leaves" at the story's outset is echoed by the "red leaves" the narrator picks off his shoes in the penultimate paragraph, at the moment he realizes what he has lost by entrusting his youth to John Baldwin. The leaves suggest home, what the narrator thought John Baldwin didn't want, and in their autumnal form they are symbols of his own lost youth. First, though, the leaves are simply realistic details. A Seager symbol suggests, it does not convey, meaning, and it never distracts the reader from the essential story.

"This Town and Salamanca" illustrates the characteristic Seager reliance upon "things" to amplify meaning. Seager believed that two things contributed most to the quality of an individual's life: imagination and objects, the dream and the thing. His fiction reflects this belief. He became aware of his own love of "surfaces" at Trudeau, and after discussing John Keats's illness with Edmund Blunden, Seager remarked in his notes: "Keats has the same love of the object—the surface—that I have."[5] That love dominates "This Town and Salamanca."

The story presents two recurring Seager concerns: the dreamers who try and live through other people and fail and the foolishness of trying to escape "this town." In Seager's fiction men fail to live their dreams for a number of reasons. Some are caught up in the manufactured dreams of the twentieth century, the dreams created by Hollywood and Madison Avenue. Others simply relive the dreams of their forebears, unable to imagine a new reality of their own. Similarly, in Seager's works migration is never a remedy for an unsatisfactory life. John Baldwin is happy not because he has traveled widely, not because he has been an adventurer, but rather because it is his own dream he has lived, and because his life has always been lived in the present—his present.

The story is autobiographical. Seager's notes show that. He, too, was a world traveler who returned to settle in "this town." And considering the story from the biographical standpoint, it is interesting that in this second story, as in his first, a man does, in a way, conquer death. John Baldwin enters the ship's hold alone, and he alone prepares and delivers the dead. He ventures into Death's kingdom and survives, just as Seager did when he entered Trudeau with tuberculosis.

Vanity Fair Fare

Seager's next published story was "Pommery 1921." It was published by *Vanity Fair*, though Seager had begun it in England. His next twelve stories were written specifically for *Vanity Fair*, and although only "Fugue for Harmonica" is in the same class with "This Town and Salamanca," a number of the stories are good. And they do deal with most of the major concerns exhibited by Seager in his fiction. Perhaps because he began writing late in life, Seager's direction remained constant. It was never a question of discovering what he wanted to say, only of developing and amplifying it.

Over and over Seager's characters try to gain control of their own lives. "Nothing can bring you peace but yourself," might well be the Emersonian distillate if one were to boil Seager's works down to a maxim. These first stories show it, and they show as well the process many a Seager character must go through: the cycle of illusion, disillusionment, and coming to awareness. Of course, not every character reaches the final stage of the cycle, and not every protagonist progresses beyond the first stage, but those characters who succeed in gaining control of their lives must go through the cycle.

Mr. Peavey, protagonist of "Pommery 1921," goes through the cycle, but Seager retreats from the implications of his growing awareness in the interests of a "twist" in the plot. This story is, according to Hugh Kenner, "a miniature of the defects of the Seager method" because it "exposes his very great talent for manipulation of detail to the demands of a mousetrap plot."[6] This is, in fact, the major fault of most of the twelve stories written for *Vanity Fair*. Seager kowtows to plot, submitting his talents and concerns to the dominance of the O. Henry twist.

Thus Peavey, the Mittyesque character desperately lacking the *savoir faire* he thinks he has, is brought to the very edge of awareness. That edge illuminates Seager's craftsmanship, for at that moment it is clear that the

point of view he selected—third person with flashes of interior monologue—is all that stands between a good story and a cheap laugh at a
pitiful character whose magazine-derived *savoir faire* fails him. The
derailment of Peavey's illusion by the reality of a dull evening among
strangers, and by the disappointing taste of champagne, is only temporary. He gets himself back on the same old track when he impresses
Hazel at the office the next morning by recounting, not his dull evening,
but his fantasy affair—the evening as he had expected, dreamed, it
would be. Thus the twist: Peavey's retreat from awareness back into
illusion has its desired effect upon reality. He does impress Hazel.

"Command Performance," like many of the early stories, is dominated by plot. Doc McCreary is a doctor-turned-beggar who prides
himself on the acting ability that enables him to be "a poor infirm old
man, ailing and dismayed," and to produce tears at will—his special
talent. Doc's act is effective, but when after a run of bad luck gambling,
he really needs money, the tables are turned: "he trembled violently and
real tears ran down his cheeks into his beard. He was not thinking about
Hamlet or how piteous he looked. He was giving a fine sincere performance with no one watching him."[7] Doc receives no reward for his sincere performance while he was once amply rewarded for fake despair. The
story is slick because its cleverly manipulated reversal ultimately dominates one's response to it.

In "Sacrament" the reliance is upon situation rather than plot, and as a
result, the characters are less wooden. The story suggests the complex
forces that can paralyze an individual's will. Joe's longing for a son
becomes confused with his sense of duty to his Church. Consequently, he
manages to have his mother-in-law committed to an asylum so that he
can afford a child. While a trifle melodramatic, the story is well
constructed: the mother-in-law's helplessness at the story's end parallels
Joe's situation at the beginning. As "Sacrament" shows, Seager wrote
better when he concentrated upon character and situation rather than
plot.

"Fugue for Harmonicas" is doubtless the best story Seager wrote for
Vanity Fair, and it is one of the best in *The Old Man of the Mountain*. The
story is firmly rooted in an experience Seager had in East Hanney; he
reshaped events recorded in his journal rather than creating them from
his own imagination. Since he didn't have to rely on plot, translating a
"real" incident into fiction as he was, his characterization was superb.
But "Fugue for Harmonicas" is also a triumph of form.

The story imitates the ternary form generally aassociated with the
classical fugue: exposition, development, and a summarizing or par-

tially recapitulating climax. The exposition: purposeless unemployed on the village green; development: Jack's new purpose and departure from the green through Cyril and Cyril's subsequent death; recapitulation: Jack's resigned return to the green. The story meets the contrapuntal requirement of the fugue—not actual counterpoint, of course, but rather a Huxleyan situational counterpoint. Seager attempted to imitate the sequence of the fugue, the various voices, through a manipulation of perspective. The narrator alternates between present and past tense in the development: "Jack Haines was unemployed," "The pump is outside," "When Cyril has played," "The recital takes an hour," "It had been very bad with Jack." In addition, "woulds" and "ifs" and the "should have spoken" of the narrator are interwoven with the predominantly past-tense presentation.

The story is once again about the forces that control a man's life. Jack gains and loses control of his life—he gains and loses purpose—entirely by chance. In addition, "Fugue for Harmonicas" suggests a generalization that appears to hold true for Seager's fiction: the more solid the autobiographical foundation, the better his fiction is likely to be. This is certainly true of the *Vanity Fair* stories, and that Seager's forays into the realm of pure imagination become more and more rare would indicate that he was aware of the fact.

The Rest of *The Old Man of the Mountain*

"Pro Arte" is one of Seager's best stories; its germ came directly from his experience. Henry Comstock is an American type, whose "cloistral naiveté" is destructive. Comstock, as the name suggests, is puritanically moral; "Pro Arte" explores the essential selfishness of his "moral" behavior. The story provides insights into a complex issue as the narrator, who is Comstock's roommate in a tuberculosis sanitarium, tries to make Comstock aware of his own selfishness; yet Comstock's primary value to the narrator is entertainment, distraction from the boredom of a slow death.

"Pro Arte" exists in an unpublished version which Seager claimed to prefer. It was five pages longer, and the major difference is that Comstock dies in the unpublished version because his conscience cannot handle the guilt once the narrator makes him aware of his own selfishness. In the published version his only guilt comes from an illicit love affair with the girl from whom he contracted tuberculosis. He began the love affair, so he told himself, to save an American pianist's budding career and shaky marriage by removing him from the clutches of his mistress. In actuality, he is merely justifying his own desire to sin. Comstock's death makes the narrator's selfishness more chilling, for he comments on Comstock's good value as entertainment after mentioning his death. However, Seager rewrote and shortened the story at the request of *Scribner*'s editors.

"Berkshire Comedy" is a preview of the light mood of *A Frieze of Girls*. It also has the tone of reminiscence that dominates the stories in that collection. As with "Fugue for Harmonicas," Seager consciously imitated a musical form. His notes show that he meant to approximate a sonata. The story is set in an East Hanney pub; the characters are English country people. Old Skinner, an aged earthy Wife of Bath, is a participant in the pub's social life in the first movement of the story. This section tells the story of Mrs. Chris, who with the help of Creepy Terry cuckolds her husband. The second movement of Seager's sonata describes Old Skinner's courtship with Jack. He plays darts for her favors. Finally, the story of Mrs. Chris is restated through Jack's jealousy, as Jack expresses fear that his beloved might turn out like Mrs. Chris: "And Jack thought she would turn out like her, did he, a great, lovely harlot? Lovely. And her sixty-three next Michaelmas with no teeth in her head and there was her legs all covered with verikus veins and Jack thought she was lovely and all the men wanted her like Mrs. Chris. Suddenly in the candlelight, Skinner began to laugh, rocking back and forth, hugging herself, laughing" (124). The story is an artful presentation of evening pub life as well as an examination of human emotions unchanging, undimished by age.

"Jersey, Guernsey, Alderney, Sark" is a serious look at a young man who is losing his grip on reality. Charles, the protagonist, foreshadows Walter Phelps of *The Inheritance*. He suffers from the same need to avenge himself against those he feels are dishonoring a dominant father's memory. Charles, like Walter Phelps, is modeled directly after a friend of Seager's who was undergoing a similar breakdown as the story was being written.

In the 1940s Seager had begun to write more stories for market value than for artistic value, first supporting his desire to write novels, then defraying the expenses connected with Barbara's illness. Six of the stories he wrote in the 1940s, however, Seager collected in *The Old Man of the Mountain*. In addition to "Jersey, Guernsey, Alderney, Sark," Seager selected "The Conqueror," a story of a young soldier just out of basic training who gets drunk and belts a blind man in a bar. The incident makes him aware "that he was still a boy and still afraid." Seager included "Game Chickens" in both *The Old Man of the Mountain* and *A*

Frieze of Girls. It is based on his first job in Memphis, for an egg case filler company. The narrator's flat tone of reminiscence, details of his summer's reading, his plans, and the nature of egg case fillers are all given equal importance, and this adds force to his account of the foreman's reaction the day a female Negro at the plant slits the throat of one of her rivals. The foreman values his game cocks more than these black human beings; in fact, the dead woman is not worth five minutes' disruption of the day's work.

"The Bang on the Head" indicts academia. Eggleston once "intended to be a scholar," but he has become obsessed with petty competition and jealousy: the seventy-five-dollar raise a colleague receives drives him to despair and to a realization that, undetected, his values have shifted tremendously. "Quitandinha" (original title: "The Pictures") is based on an incident in Brazil when Seager's daughter, Mary, contracted dysentery and nearly died. In the story the illness serves to focus Hadden Carter's mind on the nature of reality: "There were no safe places. You could neither go to them nor construct them artificially" (34). This realization leads Carter to regard his once-precious camera as unimportant and, for the first time in his wife's memory, to discipline his daughter. Because death has intruded on his drama Carter appreciates reality more fully.

"No Son, No Gun, No Streetcar" concerns a father who confides to the boy who loves his daughter that his own dreams of becoming an architect were shattered by his marriage, that he would, in fact, trade his lovely daughter, fine wife, and lucrative business for the opportunity to be an architect. The story is good, but again too much attention is given to the twist in the plot: the boy expected the father to "force" him to marry his daughter yet receives the unexpected urgent advice that he not do so.

"Sham" won the five-thousand-dollar first prize in the 1947 College Faculty Short Story Contest, but only because, unknown to him, Seager's wife had mailed the manuscript in to *Good Housekeeping*. "Sham" was retitled "The Old Man of the Mountain" for inclusion in the anthology, and it is one of Seager's best. It is in many ways a preface to *Amos Berry*. Hank Childreth is an eighty-six-year-old farmer who, as a child, saw Jesse James. When Hollywood descends on the Ozarks to make a movie about the James boys, tourists descend along with them. Old Hank is disgruntled by the rude and silly tourists, and he questions the behavior of grown men who shove horses off an eighty-foot cliff into a river. Smashing horses doesn't worry him; he is outraged because the movie company lies about Jesse James. He has no sympathy for Jesse's memory, simply a high regard for the truth.

When tourists swimming in the creek scare his mules with firecrackers, Hank—already irritable—drives them off his land with a shotgun. In the interests of the new prosperity, and out of fear that the relative of a powerful state politician has been offended, a delegation from town tries to persuade Old Hank to let the tourists back on his land to see the cave where the movie was shot. Hank drives them away, firing his shotgun over their heads and yelling, "God damn the whole twentieth century" (180).

The story is beautifully crafted. Hank Childreth's father once confronted the James boys trying to steal his horses, and this anecdote is nicely contrasted with the movie company's treatment of horses as well as Hank's own attitude toward animals. A subplot involves the daughter of a local barber running away with a cowardly braggart of a stuntman. The barber's attitude toward the prosperity the movie is bringing his town changes because of his personal involvement. Hollywood dreams are glorious from a distance, but, in fact, they corrupt and destroy.

Seager wrote four stories especially for inclusion in *The Old Man of the Mountain*. "All Problems are Simple" is essentially a character study. An Assistant Dean counsels a student, a World War II veteran, disturbed by a wartime atrocity. The veteran is haunted not by the victim, but by the men who committed it because he reasons "a man has more in common with any other men than he has differences." The Assistant Dean is worried, not about doing his job, but about the possibility of lunching with the Vice-President. Not only is the student's plight ignored, but the student's concern with a universal question concerning the nature of man is of no interest to the career-minded Dean. It is a wickedly believable portrait of an all-too-typical academic administrator. It implies that evil can be banal as well as violent.

"Flight South," echoing Seager's jarring childhood transplantation, is a slight story about a boy who has moved north and desperately wants to return home. He secretly orders a Superman costume and jumps from a second-story window in an attempt to fly south. Yet another story about the alteration of thought by modern media, this one suffers from too much reliance upon plot.

"Kobold" is another delightful character study. There is really no plot; it simply deals with an eccentric drunkard who has an unreturnable serve, and who could have beaten Tilden or Budge were it not for a thirst so strong that he carried bottles of almond extract with him for alcoholic emergencies.

"The Unicorn," the last story in the collection, rivals "This Town and Salamanca" as one of Seager's best. "The Unicorn" is also a wonderful companion piece to the earlier story. Ellen Catesby is a wealthy widow in a small midwestern town. An Englishman, Antony Braithwaite, suddenly appears in "this town"—pronouns again, no proper nouns—and attaches himself to Ellen. Soon after proposing marriage to her, he commits suicide. The story is much greater than the bare bones of the plot suggest. On one level, in fact, it is a reversal of the old Henry James confrontation between the young Republic and old, experienced Europe.

In "The Unicorn" the cultured European has fled to America because in England a man's "dossier is more important than he is." And Ellen Catesby is "using" Tony Braithwaite as certainly as he is using her. She is using him to entertain herself; she is using him to affront "this town": "She had been taught to despise them and it did not occur to her—how could it?—that these were the people she wanted to impress. She had not learned that her life was rich only as theirs was stupid and monotonous, by contrast" (267).

She is using him to give her life meaning, and when he commits suicide, Ellen, too, considers taking her life: "She looked down at the capsules in her hand. She was too young for them. The republic was not old enough" (278). While Ellen is tired, because of the strength she received from her forebears who "plowed with oxen" she is not as tired as Tony. While she and Tony both live in the past, he is too weak to take a step into "a future however sure." She is not.

The weight of history is too great for Tony, and while the past does confine Ellen Catesby to a certain extent, she still has the possibility of reactivating her will, the hope of taking herself in hand and making yet another beginning. Tony is knowledgeable, glamorous, and ultimately weak. While the system that produced Ellen has made her innocent and, by comparison, ignorant, the future is possible for her. For Tony only the past is possible: he can't conceive of a life other than the one to which he was born.

The portrait of the Englishman of good family who has fallen on hard times is convincingly exact, as is the characterization of the *nouveau riche* Ellen Catesby who, in spite of her impeccable education, wide travel, and fancy house, is still "a small-town girl." "The Unicorn" abounds with the delightful details that characterize Seager's best fiction: Baron Gustav von Stolp has a lobster in his golf bag because the lobster is wrapped, and "officers are not seen carrying parcels," Braithwaite's blue Guards overcoat has "long leather-lined pockets, 'for carrying whiskey in,'" and Right Honourables are, of course, "the younger children of earls and marquesses."

"The Unicorn" is a story about Europe and America, and about the death of the will. It depicts the debilitating effect the past can have on the present. At the same time it is a delightful private joke. Braithwaite was Allan Seager's middle name, and Tony's hands, as well as most of his amusing anecdotes, are Seager's. And yet Ellen has Seager's grandfather and his house in Tecumseh. She certainly has the attitude he had toward the people with whom he grew up. Seager portrays himself confronting himself, as it were. "The Unicorn" is one of those rare and superb stories that function as impressively on a personal level as they do on a universal level. It is a small masterpiece in which the master has slyly included a recognizable likeness of himself.

Truth with the Feel of Fiction

Seager's second collection of short fiction is a collection with a special focus: the stories are admittedly autobiographical, as the subtitle indicates, and they are a chronicle of youth from a distance provided by age. *A Frieze of Girls*: *Memoirs as Fiction* was published in 1964, and it was an early example of a trend toward "nonfiction novels," of which *In Cold Blood* and *The Executioner's Song* are characteristic examples.

The collection has unity; the stories cohere, primarily because the narrator is recognizably consistent from story to story: he is an experienced and thoughtful individual looking with amusement at himself as a young man, seeing as humorous the very things his younger self approached with over-inflated seriousness. The distance between Seager's memories and his fiction was never great, and these stories do explore old ground. American culture is examined, and Seager concludes that Americans are not the "faceless conformists" sociologists conjure up, rather Americans, "one by one, are a strange people." The English, he declares, are likely to be types more often and eccentrics less often than Americans. America provides the scope for a greater variety of experiences than does England, and these stories present that variety through the eyes of one young man—though reflected through his older self.

Nearly every reviewer concluded that *A Frieze of Girls* was good entertainment. A clean split, however, arose on the question of the book's worth. The mixed reaction is part of a larger disagreement about the aims and values of fiction. Although some reviewers rejected Seager's use of abundant detail, Seager, quoting Lionel Trilling, suggested that details were to American fiction what manners had been to British fiction, that, in fact, in the United States details were ultimately manners. And when reviewers rejected entertainment as an important element of fiction, they rejected the average reader. Seager's fiction was never aimed exclusively at an intellectual or literary elite. He wanted the average man to read and to be changed by the experience. Pure entertainment was merely diversion, of course, but entertainment could be effective strategy as well.

Finally, some reviewers felt the protagonist was too smug and priggish. Seager readily confessed to being a bit of a prig as a young man; however, he was bothered that educated men would, on the basis of a protagonist's attitude ("smug," "a long brag"), ignore the inherent worth of examining that individual's life. Any life, Seager declared, was interesting and potentially valuable. As Seager once said of a thoroughly despicable individual who lied to him and tried to deceive him: "Now he interests me, and like all people who interest me, he can't offend me."[8]

One reviewer discourses on "novelists" and mistakenly attacks Seager for a "longish prefatory defence of a novel on irrelevant points,"[9] whereas Seager actually treats the relationship between truth and fiction, never mentioning novels. The reviewer's confusion is understandable if not justifiable. The stories (some call them "sketches") are joined, albeit loosely, because they concern the youth of a single character, and because they are set against a fascinating era in recent American history—from the last years of the Jazz Age to the Great Depression.

The first three stories are a record of Seager's high school years in Memphis, the next four chronicle the undergraduate at Michigan. The eighth story—the best in the collection—is "The Old Man," an oblique view of Seager through an unsentimental examination of his grandfather. The last five stories take the narrator through his Rhodes Scholarship, Oxford, and a battle with tuberculosis. Seager presents himself as unflinchingly as he does the characters in his earlier fiction, and it is clear that he fights the same battles they do. Beneath the smug, flippant, and even hedonistic surface of the character Allan is a serious mind and a spirit that needs to soar.

The stories display the strands of the web that traps an American youth with a developing aesthetic sensibility: the social, historical, and personal elements that are woven into it, as well as the odd filaments of pure bad luck, such as illness and being in the wrong place at the wrong time.

"Under the Big Magnolia Tree" is an amusing introduction to the narrator Allan who is pursuing the woman of his dreams—a frequent activity in *A Frieze of Girls*. In the course of his hilariously unsuccessful pursuit of the beautiful Helen, the narrator sketches the milieu of the day in satisfying detail: the strict ritual of the dance, including the proper methods of drinking, dancing, and fighting; the sinister implications of improper modes of transportation; minutiae of Mississippi River swimming races.

"Powder River in the Old Days" follows Allan to his uncle's ranch in Wyoming, and the narrative is an apparently straightforward account of Allan's introduction to cowpunching and his need, once again, to impress a beautiful girl slightly older than himself. But for all its easy flow, the story is also an account of the clash between East and West, between twentieth-century urban values and the frontier.

"Game Chickens," although reprinted from *The Old Man of The Mountain*, does belong in *A Frieze of Girls*. Its position following two whimsical stories heightens the impact of this look at the twisted values that allow a man to care more for chickens than other humans.

"Dear Old Shrine Our Hearts Round Thee Twine" takes Allan to the University of Michigan, and the reader follows a merry path through the college rituals of the time: drinking and buying bootleg whiskey, finding the "right" fraternity, beating the system in the classroom, pursuing girls. The story is light and funny, but it has serious implications. The compulsion to drink was "one of the *rites de passage*," but "unlike those of the Sioux or the Trobrianders," the undergraduate's "rites went drearily on and on, year after year." This observation has been made by anthropologists as well, and Joseph Campbell, for one, has explored the sinister consequences of these indefinite rites. Seager deals with the consequences in his fiction, too, especially in *The Inheritance*. And of long discussions of techniques for seducing girls, Seager observes, "Is there any American who does not believe that there is a technique for everything? As a people we believe in the foolproof recipe."[10] Seager's novels explore the ramifications of this seemingly innocuous observation—the sinister aspects of Americans' exaggerated expectations is at the heart of *The Inheritance* and *Amos Berry*.

"The Nicest Girl in Cook Country" is basic Americana: glimpses of the prohibition-era underworld. Allan's roommate dates the sister of a Chicago bootlegger; it is barely accurate to refer to the storyline as a plot. In fact, it is primarily an account of the distance between Allan's stereotyped vision of big-time gangsters and the gradual reality he discovers. Bone Egan, for example, was "about five-nine and looked like a harassed young executive." Eventually Bone is killed by rival gangsters, but the narrator wonders about Bone's sister, Sara, who was "in the calm center of this vortex, reading Gide, conducting her Reimannian equations thoughtfully, knowing exactly where the money came from, yet, with an almost aristocratic confidence, never seeming to be afraid" (*FOG*, 94). The story is a character study, a group portrait, which counterpoints the college boys, their views of gangsters, and the reality of the bootleggers, who are merely entrepreneurs, businessmen in the best American tradition, but with the added dimension of inherent personal danger. And at the heart of the story is the aristocratic Sara.

"Actress with Red Garters" is also basically a character study. Allan dates Marta van de Puyl—actress, honor student, unconventional intellectual—who reacts against her well-to-do parents and their conventional values. She plans to marry, but for one month only, in order to get to New York City, and she does so. Finally, she marries a black man and accompanies him to Russia. While the story probes Marta's character, it also reveals the narrator's. Marta's behavior reveals to Allan his own misconceptions about intellectual females, beautiful women, and seduction. A double-edged character study, the story is delightful for its details as well: the drinking rituals, the myriad particulars of proper undergraduate behavior, the brief sketch of Bing Crosby as a Rhythm Boy with the Paul Whiteman Band. The character of the era is gradually revealed in these stories.

"Miss Anglin's Bad Martini" is an extended anecdote interlarded with anecdotes, all of them related to the hazards of drinking during prohibition. It is probably the lightest story in the collection, but once again its details please: descriptions of movie serials, Pastor Russell of the Jehovah's Witnesses, jail cells in Memphis, and slang—"Ride 'em," says the hotel cop.

If "Miss Anglin's Bad Martini" is the closest thing to pure fluff in *A Frieze of Girls*, the story which follows it, "The Old Man, a Nineteenth-Century Steel Engraving," is clearly the best. The story is elegant and eloquent. It is carefully structured, opening with the moment Allan learns of his grandfather's death and ending with something approaching understanding of the Old Man's character, an understanding which had eluded Allan because he was unable to see beyond his grandfather's apparently close-fisted, mean-spirited style.

The Old Man's children don't grieve for him because he was so hard on them: fifteen-year-old Maude fainted pushing back hay in hot weather and was allowed to rest the fifteen to twenty minutes it took to get the next load up; Arch's hand was scarred by a bullwhip cut when he was ten years old, an incentive to plow straight furrows; Maude lugged wool across the cold ground to the creek because the Old Man had to catch the Boston market early; Mac, now dead, was mistreated in some fashion so cruel that the Old Man's children have never spoken of it to anyone else.

Yet, as the story makes clear, it was just such men as Bowman Seager the country needed to tame the frontier. Bowman had started with a "chaos of walnut trees," but he had peopled the land and made it prosper. "The hatred and any random joys were irrelevant. They had glanced off him" (*FOG*, 158). Allan thus finds clues to the nation's character as well as his own. "The Old Man" is a meaningful companion piece to Seager's novels, for their protagonists are shaped by ancestors in Bowman Seager's mold.

Allan's desire to get to Europe is the focus of "The Scholarship." He makes a mistake many of Seager's characters make, ignoring completely the nature of his professors who have traveled in Europe, because he is "dazzled by where they had been." The account of Allan's maneuverings after he has applied for a scholarship are as whimsical as they are revealing. He must arrive at the proper persona, but is it the athlete, the intellectual, or the leader of men? The distance between the real and the adopted personality parallels the gap between the dream of Europe and the reality, something which is hinted at in the mundane examination before the scholarship selection committee.

In "The Drinking Contest" the narrator is at last in England. The story opens with a brief sketch of his English-born maternal grandfather, John Allan, who "wore a zinc insole in one shoe and a copper one in the other to seize terrene electricity and conduct it to his rheumatics." The story is interlarded with details of Oxford and anecdotes of the Oxford manner, but the kernel of action is brief. It is an account of Allan's victory over an officer of the Brigade of Guards in a drinking contest. The contest serves to open Allan's eyes. Despite his maternal grandfather, "England was not the old home after all. It was a foreign country where you lived among strangers" (*FOG*, 190).

At the story's center is a contrast of national character. An American, for example, is apt to tell his life story to a complete stranger, possibly "a hangover from the frontier where every man appeared as a free-standing individual unencumbered by a personal history and so had to identify himself, sometimes by bragging" (*FOG*, 184). An Englishman, however, reveals his class by his speech, his "school, college, or regiment" by his necktie; he is identified by his trappings. "The Drinking Contest" continues the collection's dual revelation: the reader knows the narrator better (because the narrator has shared some newly acquired self-knowledge) and he has also acquired a deeper understanding of American culture through the narrator's self-revelation.

American and English attitudes are contrasted once more in "The Joys of Sport at Oxford." Here the English have one of their few clear-cut victories in *A Frieze of Girls*. The casual English approach to training, the prevailing attitude that sport should be fun, makes the narrator aware of "how far morality had invaded sports in the U.S."

"The Cure" might be subtitled "a light-hearted look at tuberculosis," even though it does hint at the somber undercurrent of sanitarium existence. The light tone is certainly appropriate to *A Frieze of Girls*. The narrator, separated from the incident he describes by time, at last comprehends the undercurrents; he understands, too, the depths of human generosity, exemplified in the crude joke of his friend George Kelly who, with two other patients, has come to see Allan off after his release from the hospital. He points at two long pine boxes and says, "Well, you won't be going alone." The desperate attempt at humor is a courteous attempt to relieve the narrator of any guilt he may have at escaping the disease while his friends remain in its deadly grip. This story is especially interesting, as well as meaningful, when compared to the losing battle Eddie Burcham fights with the same disease in *The Inheritance*.

The final story, "The Last Return," accounts, in an oblique way, for *A Frieze of Girls*. It supplies the details of Allan's return and of his examinations, but the primary focus is the four-month period between the completion of exams and the resumption of his education in October. He spends it writing, and the product is, of course, "The Street." Thus the collection ends with Allan Seager, writer, returning to America. "The Street" marked the beginning of Seager's career as a writer; it was, appropriately, the first story in *The Old Man of the Mountain*. That the last story in Seager's final collection of stories accounts for the genesis of "The Street" establishes a neat symmetry.

The Best of the Rest

It is a neat symmetry, though, only when one considers the two collections of short fiction, for outside these collections lie a number of Seager stories as good as many that were collected. "The Musical Saw and Pygmalion the Less," is one, for example. It is an hilarious account of a husband and wife who, aided by "a rather large grant from a foundation," attempt to teach an ape to speak by raising it as if it were a human child—Tarzan reversed. Seager savages quasi-scholarship throughout his fiction, and this story complements the dinner scene involving the eighteenth-century specialist in *Amos Berry*, as well as such stories as "The Great Turtle Migration," "A Bang on the Head," "All Problems are Simple," and "Colorless in Limestone Caverns."

"It's Hard to Recognize a Drowning Man" foreshadows *Death of Anger*. Henry Rattigan sees a man "actually begin to drown" in the midst of "stumbling, shouting, half-swimming people fifteen feet from shore." He saves him easily, much to the admiration of the other swimmers. When he returns to his squalid home life and the wife he no longer loves, the metaphor is clear. "A drowning man is almost invisible for some reason," and he has been drowning for ten years in his marriage. The story's only weakness is that it goes a few sentences too far with the dramatic implication that Rattigan plans to drown his wife.

Most of Seager's later stories are noteworthy, but some are clearly superior. "A Whole Hundred Points Against" is a psychological study of a man who can no longer control his life. He is sane enough to handle things but disturbed enough not to want to. That so many later stories, as well as the final novel, deal with a man who is nearly paralyzed by bad fortune and despair is understandable considering the facts of Seager's life during the composition of these later works—especially the fact that his wife was in the final stages of her struggle against multiple sclerosis. The protagonist's fortuitous "accident" in "A Whole Hundred Points Against" oddly foreshadows Seager's own at the *Esquire* Writers Conference.

"The Enchanted Princess" is a modern fairy tale about a man who has lost his wife in an accident and who travels to see the woman he has loved since youth. Ironically, when the golden dream of his youth, the "enchanted princess," is destroyed by his meeting with the real, aged and alcoholic woman, the protagonist recovers his zest for living; his magical transformation is accomplished by the shattering of the vision from the past because once it no longer has a hold on him he can enjoy the present and, it is assumed, the future.

"One Jaguar Shot Dead" explores the old Seager theme: one can never escape one's roots. It examines the emptiness and loneliness of a well-to-do youth who tries to reject "money, possessions, even history along the way, a foolish impossibility because they all stick like glue."

Seager's last stories range from despair to hilarity. In "The Rope" he studies the human mind's resources through the ability of a prisoner to survive in maddening isolation. "The Good Doctor" fires one last volley at spurious research. Dr. John Tenario "nursed fierce ambitions for fame and fortune," so he set about inventing a disease. Soon after his article describing the disease appears in the *United States Journal of Medicine*, people begin developing its symptoms. Fame and television appearances follow quickly. Tenario contracts his own imaginary disease, and with a final deft twist, Seager sends him limping off to the laboratory, undaunted, to make his fortune from an invented and imaginary cure.

Seager's last published story, "Colorless in Limestone Caverns," appeared in *Playboy* five months after his death. Reinhart has quickly climbed the ladder of academic success by experimenting, somewhat callously, on animals. When blind cave fish arrive for his latest experiment, Reinhart becomes lost in admiration for them. They are self-sufficient; they have adapted their nerves themselves, with no one's help. Reinhart, absorbed in the fish, loses his ambition; in fact, his life becomes rather like that of his fish. He is calm, relaxed, and he reacts only to direct stimuli. He soon regards the fish as superior beings, innocent, living in peace. They have produced no "Rome, Germany, and other abominable crimes."

The story ends ambiguously. With an effort Reinhart reenters his old world; he resumes his research, he fathers a son, he once again drives to get ahead. Within a year the fish are dead. The reader is left to judge the nature of Reinhart's triumph; in Reinhart's life meaning would appear to be where he finds it. Perhaps, then, a meaningful life is only a matter of perspective: Reinhart immobile and watching the fish could be as meaningful as Reinhart frantically guiding his future by churning out articles on them. It matters not how an individual controls despair, that he does control it is sufficient. That is triumph.

Clearly, Allan Seager controlled his despair by writing. The crises of his own life are transmuted into the crises of his protagonists; this is especially clear in his last few stories. The artist faces down the incredibly powerful forces of despair for the reader as well as for himself. The best of Seager's stories do just this.

Chapter Three
Equinox
The Place to Say Things

Allan Seager felt a sense of responsibility as a novelist that was much more solemn and inflexible than, after his first few stories, what he had felt as a short story writer. The novel was the place to "say" things, and the more important and urgent the things to be said, the larger the necessary framework: "I have been staring at my notes for a novel and I can see the framework is not big enough—that is, it does not offer enough chance to say all I want to," Seager wrote in April 1939.[1] Less than a month later he had his embracing framework and had begun to write. With the writing of *Equinox* (1943) Seager became first and foremost a novelist.

Equinox proved to be his most widely read and widely reviewed novel. Its popularity was due, in part, to its spectacular subject: incest—if only psychological—between daughter and father. The basic plot is simple enough: Richard Miles, a disillusioned foreign correspondent, returns to New York rather than witness the destruction of his beloved France at the outset of World War II. He is soon joined by his seventeen-year-old daughter, Mary who runs away from her domineering maternal grandmother to seek asylum with her father. Mary is starved for affection: she has not seen her father in ten years, her mother is dead, and she has been raised by nuns and her uncaring grandmother. Thus her love for Miles transcends the usual love of a daughter for her father. A villainous amateur psychologist, Verplanck, makes Mary aware of the special nature of her love; this sudden awareness of what she regards as a mortal sin leads inevitably to tragedy: her suicide.

While *Equinox* examines the impact of "sin" upon an innocent, its scope is much greater; the developing war afforded Seager the large framework he sought, and he makes it clear that the forces that destroy Mary Miles are the same forces that, amplified, are destroying European civilization. Most reviewers failed to see that Miles shared with Verplanck the responsibility for his daughter's death. Both confuse ends and means, and Miles's failure with his daughter parallels his public evasion of responsibility. Miles retreats from the war, and in doing so he retreats from the budding awareness that he is somehow implicated in its causes. He uses Mary as a shelter from the growing storm in Europe; and when the storm brews in his own home, he retreats again. First he ignores what he sees—as so many newsmen and politicians did with Germany; then he evades his responsibility and turns to Verplanck for help.

Standard Man, Standard Vision

In turning to Verplanck, Miles has tacitly acknowledged an insidious notion, "standard man," whose emergence he has deplored. Though Seager had an intense interest in psychology and kept up on developments in the field to the end of his life, he was hesitant about granting it respectable scientific status. He declared that psychology was "an ex post facto business," and that it put down "too simple a frame" over everything "after the acting and thinking is done." He admired the effort to lay down rules, but believed that human beings were too complex to justify most of the conclusions of the psychologists: "We are not the same people at all idle as we are working, hungry or full, lying down or standing, I'm damned if I don't think we have a set of values for every hour of the day. Why, then, take something that is probably just a phase and act and think from it as if it were constant."[2]

Rather than treat Mary's behavior as special and personal, Miles entrusts her to Verplanck and his generalizations. Mary is no longer an individual, she is a "case study." She is examined via standardized vision, vision limited by the tenets of psychology. And this standardized vision is central to the woes of the modern world. Standard vision, standard man, standard behavior; as variety is limited, freedom is diminished.

Virtually all of Seager's recurrent motifs are present in *Equinox*: the individual's loss of control over his own life, the paralysis of the will, the inability of individuals to see, let alone alter, the forces controlling their lives. It has the central Seager concern: the "basic American theme" of man trying to be free. *Equinox* probes, as do Seager's subsequent novels, the nature of parenthood, the validity of modern "values," and the tyranny that, in one form or another, the past exercises over the present.

The essential theme, at its most basic level, is simply man trying to be free. Although it is fatuous to attempt a summary of any man's life with a single phrase, Seager was above all else a man consciously trying to be free. First he attempted to free himself from his environment, seeking escape through books and then "flight" to England. Gradually he discovered his freedom lay within himself, a discovery that he grants a number of his protagonists—notably Eddie Burcham, Amos and Charles Berry, and, presumably, Richard Miles. An inevitable Seager companion theme is the inability of the individual to exercise control over his own life. The tension of the two themes—seeking freedom but lacking control—produces the plot.

The Seager protagonist is, as Hugh Kenner points out, "a man acting blindly, deflected by a thousand little things, and gradually learning why he acts."[3] Usually the protagonist learns only after a conscious withdrawal from society, a failed attempt at freedom. His new self-knowledge doesn't necessarily make him free; it is only the means to possible freedom, a possibility nonexistent up to that point. Even if the protagonist is no freer than before, he is, at least, aware of the forces limiting his freedom, and recognizing these forces he has the chance to deal with them.

Withdrawing to the safety of an apartment with his daughter, shutting himself off from the troubles of the outside world, Richard Miles anticipates the attempted escapes in Seager's subsequent novels: Walter Phelps's defiant withdrawal, a rebellion that places him outside society; Amos Berry's retreat into self-sufficiency and isolation; Hilda Manning's flight from her home town; Hugh Canning's "escape" to Europe. Richard Miles is only the first protagonist of a Seager novel to learn that escape is virtually impossible. His temporary escape, like that of the protagonists who follow him, is doomed because he has not learned where the possibility of freedom lies. Seager's characters must turn inward; freedom comes from acceptance and through responsibility, not flight from responsibility. Typically Richard Miles engages in a blind struggle, striving for freedom, but as yet unaware of its location.

The source of *Equinox*'s formal strength is the tension of its oppositions. Seager's investigation of the inability of the individual to control his life is countered by his choice for a protagonist of a man struggling to be free. The forces surrounding and immobilizing his will are enumerated, and in examining them, Seager reveals potentially liberating agents. Because illusion is a powerful constraint upon the will, the conflict between appearance and reality is central to *Equinox*. Illusion assumes many forms: its assault is constant. *Equinox*'s imagery quite naturally buttresses its themes, and vision imagery pervades the novel, appropriately, since so many of the individual's problems originate from his inability to see clearly. Miles's view, for example, is limited by his journalistic training, a frame restricting his field of vision. This passive—often called objective—observation erodes the individual's control, just as it contributes to what Miles calls a "standardized vision" of events.

The Observer

Equinox's first chapter presents Miles in his customary role, the observer. Neutral, he watches his fellow travelers Loudon and Ipolyi squabble, failing to intervene when violence erupts between them. He is grateful for the distraction they provide, "they were the itch you claw to distract you from a toothache."[4] Miles observes to avoid feeling; he observes to evade examining his own motives, especially concerning his departure from Europe. Miles's condition is counterpointed by the refugees in third class who are escaping Europe to preserve themselves: escape and preservation are literal. Miles is attempting an escape, but he has no idea from what. His identity was in danger in Europe, and he flees to escape psychic extinction; his flight is a first step in a search for that identity, a quest for selfhood.

The nature of Miles's observation is revealed symbolically as the novel opens: "Smiling vacantly, his temple on his fist in a pose of courteous attention, Miles watched the porthole beyond the Hungarian's shoulder" (4). It is at this point that he thinks, "This is the equinox, the change of the weather." He can only watch the equinoctial storm "blowing up," just as he could only observe the international storm brewing in Europe. He will do no more than observe the storm blow up between Ipolyi and Loudon, just as he will do little more than observe the storm blowing up in his own life. Man must act, as Seager's protagonists learn; the individual must take himself in hand and exert his will in an attempt to gain control over his own life.

The porthole through which Miles observes the equinoctial storm brewing is paralleled at the novel's end by the window he stares out after Mary's death. Once again he gazes helplessly at the effects of the equinoctial weather (400). The storm in his private life is in many ways an extension of the storm in Europe: both are seen with limited vision, thus both are beyond control. Because they are ideal symbols of limited perspective, windows pervade *Equinox*.

Mary goes to the window and looks out on dark streets just before her suicide (386), Verplanck looks "out through the shopwindow into the darkening street full of whirling snow" when Helen informs him his plans have gone awry (201), the poet Seward Stephenson lives in a room behind a window with "ANTIQUES" lettered on it (44). *Amos Berry* and

The Glass House show that the poet is nearly alone in fighting the creation of standard man, and that both the poet and his primary weapon, his vision, are antiques, anachronisms amidst standard men and standard vision. Automobile windows are nicely linked to the limited vision created in a world of technology, most masterfully in chapter four, which contrasts Mary's concern for the eternal with the temporal, materialistic vision of the nuns, and ends with Mary beating on the station wagon windows and begging the sister to let her out.

Equinox is packed with the paraphernalia of "looking": it contains well over a hundred references to windows, mirrors, binoculars, movies, photographs, reflections in water, and the like. Mirrors naturally complement windows; they not only limit the field of vision, they reflect reality. Thus Margery, Miles's former mistress, who is all surface, finds her identity in mirrors—she is her appearance. Miles, searching for identity, has never found anything he likes in mirrors. Linked to Margery, mirrors acquire sexual connotations; e.g., the ceiling mirrors she desires for entertaining Miles and the lustful stares she encourages from the taxi driver in his rear-view mirror. Thus when Miles clandestinely watches Mary in a mirror at the Christmas party, he is once again the uninvolved observer with a limited view, and the scene at the same time reinforces the incest motif. The interplay of vision symbols is complex and satisfying; consider one final example: Mary intently searching her face for visible traces of sin, evidence of her unnatural love, in a mirror.

Miles recognizes, at *Equinox*'s end, the forces at work to immobilize his will; hope is held out for his freedom. For modern man as a whole the outlook is more bleak, for he has come to see "reality" through a succession of frames that limit and define it for him. Events are filtered through the eyes of reporters, and reporters often see through the eyes of a government—as with Miles's "conducted tour" of Warsaw. In fact, Miles, the expert and respected foreign correspondent whose opinion people seek out, has never really understood the Continent, "seeing it as a goose sees the country it flies over, going south, honking" (40). The expanding war in Europe represents the triumph of technology over the individual man; it is a monstrous impersonal force deciding the fate of millions who neither comprehend the issues nor the stakes. Ironically, neither does this man whose occupation it is to do so.

If reporting defines and limits reality, so do photographs and movies, and they do so even more insidiously. In his working notes for *Equinox* Seager wrote, "Don't forget photographs, becoming for modern man more real—a closer approximation—than his own dreams. viz. Eddie's desire for a movie star or a model."[5] Although Seager tried to make it explicit, most reviewers missed the point of the photographic session in chapter two. The transformation of a fake reality into a dream of what should be will sell dresses, and it is only one symptom of the confusion of appearance, dream, and reality. Men lust after the faked seductive expression of the movie star; women believe that wearing the same dress will transform their reality and give them the same seductiveness.

Margery compares Verplanck's marriage proposal to "talking to someone in a movie," and she visualizes the outcome of her acceptance in cinematic terms, complete with close-up, pan shot, medium shot, and montage (175). This is echoed later when Stanley Dinsmore proposes to Mary: "He wanted to do it smoothly, the way they did it in the movies" (356). Both the worldly Margery and the callow Stanley have been had by the movies; they see and act according to the standards of a fantasy world.

Movies cover a broad thematic area: it is to the Translux Theatre that Miles escapes from home once he realizes the incestuous nature of Mary's feelings. And when Mary, rushing toward suicide, sees the external world as if it is an old-time movie, the network of associations is expanded again.

Symbolic Interplay

While vision imagery clearly predominates in *Equinox*, it by no means functions in isolation. *Equinox* is a carefully interwoven fabric of plot, theme, and expanding symbols. Often symbols accrue meaning as a result of the tension of their interplay. Darkness, flowers, and illness are among the most prominent symbols, and they often overlap. Darkness is obviously fitting in a novel dominated by vision, and it acquires the multiple associations of security, blindness, and sexual desire—all ingredients of the tragedy.

Attempting to define Miles, Margery discards his surface appearance, "definitely not his clothes," and identifies him sexually: "Richard, like every man she knew, identified himself in darkness" (31). In her fateful confrontation with Margery, Mary reveals that her feelings for her father are somehow tied to darkness: "I can't explain how it is, but it is in the darkness somehow and I am with him. The heart and lungs beat in darkness safely, don't they" (185). This is indicative of the Seager method in *Equinox*. Two of the associations that darkness acquires are at work in this passage: the sexual, as indicated in Margery's thoughts, and the secure. It is also linked tangentially to the disease motif through the mention of lungs, for Mary's mother died of tuberculosis, and Grandma Harrison, foreshadowing the truth, warned Miles that he will kill Mary as surely as he killed his wife. Appropriately, after Mary's speech revealing her feelings about her father, Margery looks out the window into the growing darkness and is suddenly aware of her own limited knowledge of love.

Consider how darkness is charged with suggestion in this passage in which Mary remembers picking a water lily:

On the shore of the cove were dark trees whose shadows made the waters black, and there she was allowed to lean over the side of the flat-bottomed boat (since there was no danger), seeing first the reflection of her face, then moving the lily into the reflection, breaking it, the bland sweet fragrance rising from the water as if in the heart of the flower, even in the root trailing deep below there were a final sweetness never yet reached, piercing and complete. . . . (134)

The memory is prompted by water lily buds her father has brought her, and it is preceded by her contemplation of this joyful new existence with her father: "She was like her father all right, an inheritance now proved but never explained in biology class. All they said there was that a planted seed grew into a flower." And considering this relationship, she concludes, "To love is to serve, said the nuns. This was love then." Despite her happiness, the assurance that she has love, something is lacking. "She had come for something else. She could not feel it or say what it was. Like a name you know but cannot remember" (133).

The lilies become explicit sexual symbols:

"Tomorrow if I wait," she thought, "it will have blossomed white and yellow. If I wait." She bent over the opening flower and sniffed, but the scent was as it had always been, mild and inconclusive. She encircled the bud with her thumb and forefinger and pushing back the green of the pod, blew into the petals. "Open, damn you," she whispered. "I can't wait any more. Open up." (134)

Here are darkness, reflection, and flowers (romance, the bouquets her father gives her; biology and explicit sexuality—the lily is a traditional symbol of purity, and the broken lily, of dishonor) interacting in one passage. The suggestions are numerous, and the power of the passage lies in its kinetic implications. Mary pulls the lily into her own reflection, the dark place is regarded as "safe" for her, and she imagines "even in the root trailing below, there [was] a final sweetness never yet reached, piercing and complete. . . ." Flowers and darkness are central to the dream-vision preceding her suicide, a final suggestion that the final sweetness, the only security, is death.

Tracing flowers throughout the novel would in itself be no small task. As explicit as the lily is, it is reinforced by flowers elsewhere; in chapter one, for example, Miles thinks of himself as "like a plant in a clay pot being carried from one soil to another, the roots and tendrils of his last bed broken and those of his destination yet to form" (17). Roots suggest both the sexual and the secure. The impulsive manner in which Miles buys the first corsage for Mary contributes to the cabbie's mistaken belief that the two are lovers, an early foreshadowing of the psychological truth. Flowers foreshadow Mary's death as well. Verplanck, in a rare moment of protective sympathy, thinks of Mary as "a flower about to be cut down." Mary's first "marriage" has its flowers. Miles feels a "spasm of pity" for Dinsmore when he sees the "red roses, flamboyant and vulgar." And Margery is identified with flowers (another sexual implication); "she was the flower [men] peeped over the edge of the rut to see" (78). Flowers are a unifying device, one of the many constants in the flux of *Equinox*, but in the area of meaning they, too, are more fluid than static.

A Careful Structure: *Trompe l'Oeil*

Equinox is tightly structured in the same sense that *Ulysses* is tightly structured. A number of reviewers complained of *Equinox*'s loose construction, its sprawl; they declared that the novel lacked unity, was "disjointed" and was "studded with short stories" barely related to the plot. In fact, Seager's use of counterpoint, foreshadowing, and echoes suggests Joyce, as does his use of juxtaposition, his implantation of real people, places, and buoyant facts into the novel. The surface chaos is appropriate to a novel set in New York, just as it is appropriate to the era: the disastrous eruption of World War II. The display of brilliantly drawn minor characters who suddenly emerge and as suddenly drop from view, the multiple points of view, is *trompe l'oeil*. Hidden beneath the shifting surface is the carefully constructed supporting structure, a meticulously crafted unity that effectively counterpoints the sprawl and jumble that is the exterior aspect of *Equinox*. This counterpoint illustrates the very theme of the novel: the inability to perceive a constant reality beyond mere surface appearance. *Equinox*'s form is appropriate to its theme.

Two of the sections that reviewers pronounced irrelevant, for example, are central to the parent-child motif. The chapter devoted exclusively to Stanley Dinsmore makes him a more sympathetic character and thus gives the elopement more credibility than it would otherwise have had. But it also complements Miles's situation, highlighting it from yet another angle. Mr. Dinsmore uses his child as selfishly as Miles uses Mary. Clearly, Verplanck's use of people is not idiosyncratic; it is a symptom of the general ill: if he does not value individuals, neither does Mr. Dinsmore, nor, in his way, does Miles. As the events in Europe demonstrate, neither do governments. The cases differ, but only in degree.

The Dinsmore section follows the chapter in which Miles and Verplanck have their long discussion of fatherhood. Both chapters investigate the mystical states of paternity and kinship, as opposed to the mere physical facts. Against these chapters the "barman's history," which most reviewers regarded as completely irrelevant, is quite apropos. The history centers on the man's father, and the climax of the long anecdote is the retort the bartender made to him: "Father? You were never a father to me. All you were was my sire" (240). The question of fatherhood is an essential ingredient of the novel; one can't read far without coming across some aspect of parenthood.

Parents, in fact, are one of the forces a person must conquer in order to exercise control over his own life. Loudon's father is an unacknowledged force in his life, and Ipolyi's insight into this fact leads to the whiskey-tossing, jaw-breaking altercation between the two. Stephenson's lack of personal control stems from his impulse to overreact to his minister father's influence, and Miles's immobile will is partially a result of his inability to overcome "daddy's rules," rules woefully inadequate in dealing with Mary's shameful love for him. Parenthood is a pervasive motif that, despite the explicit comments of an omniscient narrator, most reviewers overlooked, just as they overlooked other unifying devices. For example, the constant counterpointing of Miles's situation with that of France seems overt once it is traced throughout the novel. The ubiquitous interwined symbols reinforce the novel's concerns by constant repetition.

Equinox establishes a crucial pattern for Seager's novels: the cycle of illusion, disillusionment, and a coming to awareness which is offered as the only hope for individual freedom. The pervasiveness of illusion in the twentieth century is obvious, and the preoccupation with "seeing" that abounds in *Equinox* objectifies this fact. Disillusionment is a very gradual process, and in Miles's case it begins only with the hint of something he is unable to see, his daughter's illicit love for him: man must learn to see that which is invisible to him—yet something with which he usually co-exists. The coming to awareness follows, but it is a slow and painful process, culminating only after Mary's death—after his "safe" place has been demolished completely. Mary's is only the first of a number of deaths in Seager's novels that serve as catalysts in the cycle of coming to awareness: Todd Phelps's death in *The Inheritance*, Hilda's son's and her husband's in *Hilda Manning*, Walter Rickert's and Amos Berry's in *Amos Berry*, and Donald's in *Death of Anger*. Death is a reminder that there is no security, and the enshrinement of security as a sacred necessity is a certain block to awareness.

But enshrinement of the right to be safe, while perfectly understandable, is part of what limits human beings. It is only when Miles discovers that he is not immune from misfortune that he is able to face his problems, examine his talent, and leave for Europe to use it, one assumes, responsibly. That Seager should deem security limiting to human potential is hardly surprising, since he began to write only after he discovered he was not immune—specifically, to tuberculosis.

Man Is Not Yet Predictable

If *Equinox* offers any hope, any comfort, it is the fact that man is not yet predictable; he is not yet irrevocably standard man. Verplanck, after all, despite his empirical methods and close observation, despite his confidence in his own special abilities, is wrong about Seward Stephenson. He is unable to manipulate Margery, even though he was certain he "knew" her before their marriage and that he could gradually persuade her to accommodate his wishes and his experiments. These two failures foreshadow his failure with Mary. Verplanck is certain that Miles will disintegrate, but it is Miles who survives, in a sense even triumphs, and Mary who is destroyed. And as the novel ends, Verplanck is wrong yet another time. He is mistakenly certain that Miles has gone to meet Margery. The fact that Miles has returned to Europe is an indication that he has at least "escaped" into awareness, responsibility, and the possibility of freedom, for Margery was linked closely to his old unthinking, unseeing life, even having been his mistress in Paris before the war.

When Verplanck, certain that Miles is with Margery, has him paged, the lines "I'm sorry. We were not able to locate him," suggest that man is not yet completely predictable, not yet pinned tightly by the oppressive weight of the forces trying to level him. Ambiguous as it is, the end of *Equinox* is nearly as hopeful as any of Seager's subsequent novels, but, then, in Seager's view, ambiguity itself is a triumph of sorts in a world of categories and pigeonholes, a world of cogs and machines.

Chapter Four
The Inheritance

Accepting the Origins

The Inheritance marks Seager's return home. He knew the novel was a personal watershed: applying for a Guggenheim Fellowship in 1965, Seager declared that in the novels he wrote after *Equinox* he found his "field": "I wrote about the people I had grown up among and they seemed to me to be fair samples not only of Americans, embodying unwittingly the history of their country, but also humanity at large, and I saw that my themes were suggested by the tensions in the ambiguities of my relationship with them."[1] Seager had said the same thing earlier, but with variations: "A pleasure of middle age is the acceptance of one's origins, whatever one had pretended, however ambivalent the bonds. If I can say anything about the sources of my work, I believe they lie in the tensions of that ambivalence."[2] More brusquely, it had been, "I hated the people I came from and I wanted to find out why."[3]

The impulse to turn his fiction homeward was there all along, and since his subject was ultimately himself, his concentration upon the southeastern corner of Michigan is in no way surprising. Seager observed and wrote because he felt himself somehow apart from his friends and neighbors. His early journals show that as a young man he hated his neighbors because they seemed to be so much less than himself. They were insensitive to music and art, they were ignorant of the forces directing their lives, they were little better than automata. Their ambitions were petty: comfort, security, and the acquisition of trivial gewgaws.

Attempting to escape these Philistines, Seager learned that escape was impossible. In England, New York, and Ann Arbor he discovered that the unrealized potential, the narrow ambition, which so disturbed him was not limited to Adrian or Memphis—or even to the United States. Nor was it a malady that affected only a particular class. Educated and uneducated were afflicted; affluent people suffered from the same illness infecting the middle class.

The shift from *Equinox* to *The Inheritance* is not simply in setting. Rather the Michigan setting, the fictional reconstruction of his home territory, derives from an insight that turned his attention from effect toward cause. *Equinox* and *The Inheritance* share themes: the paralysis of the will and man's continual struggle to be free are central to both novels. But while *Equinox* concentrates upon symptoms, *The Inheritance* clearly begins to trace the complex causes of these symptoms. Where better to seek causes than where he had first reacted against the effects? Seager found his "field" at home.

Walter Phelps, the protagonist, is a near-duplicate of friends from "home," and yet reviewers weren't willing to accept the reality of Walter Phelps. Richard Match, for example, drew the line at the "painfully artificial set of private circumstances" Seager "imposed" on Walter Phelps.[4] Match's reaction is one that plagued Seager's fictional return home. Yet those *litterateurs* who attribute the "decline of fiction" to a modern condition characterized by the essential absurdity of fact may be correct, for if Walter Phelps's situation is "incredible" and "painfully artificial," so then was the situation of Phelps's real-life counterparts.

The story of Walter Phelps is essentially a telescoping of the similar situations of two of Seager's friends. Walter Phelps was, in fact, modeled so closely after one of them that Simon and Schuster's lawyers directed Seager to obtain a legal release from him before they would consider publishing *The Inheritance*: correspondences were simply too exact.

In bare outline the plot is simple enough. As a young boy Walter Phelps shouts at his best friend's father, who has just slapped him, "My father can lick you!" And at that moment his father magically appears—raging from an encounter with his employer—and with a single blow to the jaw proves his son's declaration to be true. The incident assumes mythic proportions for Walter, who is thereafter unable to escape the shadow of his father. After his parents die in an automobile accident, Walter learns that the father he has glorified is mortal: neither his financial nor his spiritual inheritance is large. Yet the more his father's image is tarnished, the more idolatrous Walter's veneration of his memory becomes. Walter then attempts to become his father, gradually assuming aspects of Todd Phelps's personality, and in an increasingly more serious series of antisocial acts, he seeks to avenge his father's memory on his home town—which had regarded Todd as a mean-spirited individual.

Eventually Walter's behavior lands him in a mental institution. Apathetically, he accedes to his Uncle Eri's wish that he commit himself, ostensibly for alcoholism. Walter is directionless, his will is paralyzed, and life in the institution is, like his life outside, primarily a matter of habit and repetition. Hope comes from his dying friend, Eddie

Burcham, who forces Walter into an awareness of his condition and thus affords him the possibility of exercising his will, of assuming responsibility for his life. His subsequent parole from the institution is a "ticket to free will." "The biggest effort" of Eddie Burcham's life has changed "Walter's flight into a search." The "coarse strength" Walter inherited from his family will enable him to break new ground now that he can "conceive of a full, decent life," a life of his own making.

The First Step toward Awareness

On its simplest level, *The Inheritance* is a detailed psychological study of Walter Phelps and, to a degree, his Athens, Michigan, neighbors. Ultimately it is an investigation into the "inheritance" of twentieth-century Americans; Seager's fictional characters, no less than his Michigan neighbors, embody "unwittingly the history of their country," and Seager's method is explicit. As Walter Phelps begins to understand the forces rendering his own will inactive, the reader, too, should begin to understand: the forces attacking Walter's will are at work upon all Americans. Walter is typical of the protagonists of Seager's novels in that Seager takes him through a cycle of illusion, disillusionment, and a coming to awareness. Seager hoped to take the reader through the same cycle. If action were ever to be possible, if the immobilized will were ever to be freed, twentieth-century man had to be led to an awareness not only of his conditions, but also of the forces that created and maintained that condition. As ever, the first step toward awareness was knowledge.

Through his own grandfather Seager had gained an explanation for the paralysis of the will he saw about him, the very paralysis he had so recently depicted in *Equinox*. Beauman Seager had taken an attitude—stern and hard—with him to Michigan from Vermont. In Vermont that attitude had been essential to survival, but the flat land in Michigan made it unnecessary. Yet Beauman couldn't change. Thus in varying ways individuals had become trapped at the intersection of past and present, and patterns of vestigial behavior rules their lives. Behavior once essential to survival had become mere habit, and human potential was suffocated in America by a "set of mind, of habits" that were "hardly a culture."[5]

"It is here in a bank, a private bank in a small town," *The Inheritance* begins, and a more apt opening sentence is difficult to imagine.[6] The antecedent of "it" is nothing less than the novel itself, for the bank, like a seed, contains the finished work: story, theme, causes, and consequences grow from the bank. The first section of the novel, set in the bank, is nearly an abstract of the novel itself. The rest is elaboration and explanation.

Near the end of *The Inheritance* Eddie Burcham tells Walter Phelps, "Dignity is better than money in the bank." Eddie then proceeds to make the theme of *The Inheritance* explicit (not for the first time): "We inherit more from our forefathers than they say on the Fourth of July. I think the tremendous effort they made . . . got into their seed and stayed there, through your grandfather and your father and maybe it's in you and me, the effort to get things. Material things were what they needed then, all kinds of things. And our families are still breaking their necks to get things, useless instead of useful now, but it only takes a part of themselves to do it. The rest withers" (333). Prefacing this proclamation with a comparison of dignity and money was clearly intentional; the end of the novel echoes its beginning.

Seager saw the bank not just as a monetary storehouse, but as a spiritual barometer, and thus as a powerful symbol. As he was writing *The Inheritance*, he wondered in his journal "how many men with nothing else to do stop in at the bank every morning to pass the time of day. If these men were in the twelfth century the same men would have probably stopped at the church for a long maundering prayer." Seager doubted that his contemporaries stopped at the bank to see if things were all right, "It is a rite, a part of their faith. Do people have a floating capacity for belief, a credulity which can be moored to whatever institution has the most prominence in their time?"[7]

In the bank, the institution of "most prominence" in this time, a critical link is forged in the chain of causes and effects shackling Walter Phelps's potential. It is in this symbol of a new faith that Todd Phelps, "hot, irritated, counting gold," attempts a "monstrous profanity" that is really a feeble and failed attempt at rebellion: he imitates a professional gambler as he counts. Todd's unsuccessful attempt at blasphemy is a vain effort to regain the dignity he is dimly aware he has lost, and his blind reflex action parallels the similar unthinking acts of defiance Walter attempts later. It is a foreshadowing of Walter Phelps's multiple inheritance.

However, Todd's impiety not only goes unnoticed but his dignity suffers further when, spurred by the impotence of his defiant gesture, he goads old man Ancil Bailey into a stinging attack upon the whole Phelps clan. An immediate effect is a blind rage which is channeled into the

right cross to John Burcham's jaw, a blow that assumes mythic proportions for Walter Phelps and ultimately has near-disastrous effects upon
his life. This first section suggests the complexity of Walter Phelps's
"inheritance," the multiple, inseparable links that will later hold his
will immobile, the intertwined causes chaining him to the past.

Ancil Bailey lashes out at Todd, angering him to the point of violence
because Todd ignores the old man's wandering soliloquy on the past, his
urgent question, "What becomes of all the changes I've seen?" (9).
Brooding over the past, Ancil Bailey suddenly employs it as a weapon in
the present. He tells Todd, "You know they used to keep a hammer
under the Gibson House bar to break the glasses your father drank out of,
don't you?" (6). And "Your mother had her feet over the dash of every
buggy in the county, in every horse barn of every little country church
every night except Sunday and Thursday prayer meeting" (10). And
finally, he curses Todd for what he is as an individual: "And never mind
your sire and dam, Goddam you for what you are, for being unkind to a
lonely old man who only wanted a minute of your time" (10). Clearly,
every man's inheritance is at once communal and individual. Walter's
eventual defiant acts against the town have as their roots a tangle of
causes both public and personal, communal and individual. The mythic
right cross that reaches into Walter's future reaches back as well,
through Ancil Bailey, into the history of the county.

The opening scene in the bank neatly envelops past, present, and the
gradual transmutation of "things" from means to end. Eddie Burcham's
explanation of the effects of ingrained habits of acquisition after the
metamorphosis of things from essential to useless is symbolically represented in Ancil Bailey's "trivial ceremony" (implying that all ceremonies
in this temple of the new faith are trivial, just as the attempted act of
blasphemy was trivial?), his daily counting of the gold. Each coin
corresponds to something remembered from his youth: wheat he has
cut, a calf he has raised, wool he has cut and sold. The essential and
meaningful "things" of Ancil Bailey's past are transformed by memory
into shining bits of inanimate matter. These pieces of metal contain the
past. The transformation is a representative, symbolic example of a
gradual, collective process.

The Tyranny of the Past

The form of the first chapter reflects the novel's theme, for in this
chapter past and present exist simultaneously. Memory breaks through
the narrative of present events again and again, even recent memory:

Todd's flashback to his morning conversation with two of the bank's stockholders, for example. A potential effect of interweaving past with present, of transforming things of the past into the present, is invested with pathetic humor: "You forgot what house you were living in when you got up at night and you bumped into the wall sometimes hunting for the door to go out back although there was a flush toilet right there in the bathroom" (4). The past warns of possible consequences of the present: "But you're getting fleshy, Todd. Ain't so trim around the waist as you were when you were doing that boxing in college." Todd understands the implied consequences well, linking them at once to his personal inheritance: "I weigh a hundred and ninety-seven. It's too fat. My uncle Paul was too fat and he died of heart trouble. My mother thinks she's going to get it and die. I'll die of heart trouble. That's what you were going to say, isn't it?" (6–7).

Seager blurs the lines between past and present. Consider the parenthetical aside in the very first paragraph, "(Yes, this is several years ago. No marble yet, all pine flooring, and in the barrier for the cashier and tellers and for panelling itself halfway up the wall, the best mahogany, nicked, dusty, solid)" (1). The narrator intrudes at the story's outset to inform the reader that the events of this first chapter and by extension, chapters two and three (completing section one of the novel), narrated as if they are taking place in the present, actually took place "several years ago." Appropriately enough, his revelatory aside consists primarily of a brief catalog of "things," signatures of the past. By interrupting, the narrator imposes the present upon the fictional past he is re-creating. And, but for his aside, he is creating a fictional present from the materials of the past as he writes, making the past exist now. Thus the narrator acts out his own theme. Story, theme, and form are nearly inextricable.

The interplay of past and present initiated at the outset of chapter one accentuates the ramifications of the novel's title at once. Elements germane to the unfolding story of Walter Phelps, and by extension to the dilemma of twentieth-century Americans, are unobtrusively present from the first. Underlying Ancil Bailey's musings on the past, and his insistent "What becomes of it?" (even as his musings illustrate his own past at work transforming his present) is another insistent question that surfaces again and again in the novel, though Bailey asks it first, "I feel as if I had been promised something and my fear is really anger, I suppose. I say, 'Is this all?' " (10). Walter Phelps takes up Ancil Bailey's question. He repeats it after his own fraternity initiation, and after his first sexual encounter, feeling each time that he has been betrayed by life, for he has waited passively for "life" to give him something intense each time.

Daniel Boorstin, in his study *The Image* (1962), a book that Seager was later to recommend to his students, suggested a decade after the publication of *The Inheritance* that modern Americans are plagued by the principle of "exaggerated expectation," a phenomenon that springs, in part, from their growing tendency to act as if their lives are controlled by some force outside themselves. [8] The irony of this debilitative passivity in a nation supposedly founded on individual initiative is obvious, and that irony echoes through Walter's feeble rebellion against convention. For his rebellion, like his conformity, is independent of his will. It is mere reflex, not unlike the reflex that sends Ancil Bailey searching for an outdoor toilet that no longer exists. Walter rebelling is no freer of the past than Walter conforming: his passive expectation and his active defiance have common roots. Both grow untended; they are not grown. Passive expectation is a predictable feature of lives based on habit rather than need.

Seager deftly uses his characters to illustrate his ideas. Eddie Burcham, forced into a passivity devoid of expectation by his illness, moves gradually toward an understanding of the self-perpetuating problem:

A part of his education had been devoted to teaching him that he, Edward Burcham, did not initiate action: he responded, like a bear in a cage, when he was poked with a stick. He also learned that what colored and conditioned his responses were his memories of events that had pleased or frightened him long ago, as a child, and the persistence of these clusters of memory gave to his thinking its form, its emphases, and its tension. He was, he thought, mainly supine, and after someone had poked him, his reactions were governed by remote control. (152)

Throughout the novel, Eddie sorts things out. Eddie (not unlike the author creating him) gains fresh perspectives because he is forced outside his environment. The early death of his father, making him slightly different from his friends, jars his perspective slightly. He sees things, to a small degree, as an outsider, as the fraternity initiation illustrates. It is, however, in the TB sanitarium, completely removed from his old life and with ample time to think, that "it grew clear to him that what had occupied his time, that long string of days begun in the obscurity of childhood, had been a habit he acquired for no reason that he knew" (214). Trivial personal examples occur to him first: he wore black stockings because "his mother had put them on him and she had put them on him because she saw other boys wearing them" (215). But eventually he makes the leap from his life to the lives of his contemporaries, from the trivial to the significant. Acquisition is a habit because, like black stockings, it has been accepted without question. And Eddie becomes aware that the primary purpose of work in America is acquisition, not survival or satisfaction.

Walter Phelps, while still in the mental hospital, comes to a similar conclusion. His realization is triggered by the simple fact that he has taken pride in his work in the asylum bakery. "He had never thought he could take any pride in the work he did here. You could adapt yourself to anything. You were living all the time. And to pretend that you could take time out, not having it count, as he was pretending his stay in the asylum did not count, was a mistake" (310). Thus Walter advances toward awareness through a simple feeling of usefulness, of pride in his work. Beneath Walter's rebellion, his attempt to "humiliate" the town, lay his own loss of dignity, a loss more imaginary than real, a loss stemming from the insult he imagines the town has done his dead father. Again, Seager's progress has been cyclical. Walter's worship of Todd Phelps, the worship moving him to avenge the insult to his father's memory, owed a great deal to that crucial blow to the jaw of John Burcham, a blow which, in turn, had its genesis in Todd's own diminished sense of dignity in his job.

The erosion of craftsmanship and pride in one's work, the reversal of means and ends, the disastrous diminishing of "work" in the twentieth century into a mere means of acquiring "things"; all of these are touched on in *The Inheritance*. In *Amos Berry* they become central. But the essential focus of *The Inheritance* is on the ingrained and repetitive actions of Americans, on habit, on automatism.

Breaking the Pattern

As he does throughout the novel, Seager neatly loops the idea so the tail of the snake is in its mouth. For Eddie uncovers the ultimate causes for the tyrannical rule of habit and proffers a possible solution, only when he himself is a slave to a particularly vicious habit. Addicted to morphine, half-blind, virtually bedridden, and probably dying, he makes his discovery. "His discovery was this: you could take yourself in hand. That was all. Somewhere, in college probably, he had picked up the notion that you were controlled entirely—he had waited for things to happen to him" (317). Eddie's conclusion, arrived at in circumstances which make its personal application highly improbable (for the arena in which he can exercise his own will has shrunk almost entirely away), echoes a line of Theodore Roethke's, a line that Seager quoted often: "The only death is the death of the will."[9] But Eddie has taken himself in hand—he is after all dying at home, not in the sanitarium to which society prefers to remove the dying from its sight and to hold false hope before them until the end. Eddie's stoic acceptance of his condition and resolution simply to continue are indications of a will revived. In fact, his conclusion that the will can triumph over habit is in itself a small victory for the will. He has learned to think with originality, escaping the deep-rutted patterns of thought he formerly accepted.

Eddie's emphasis upon habit is central to *The Inheritance*, for habit is the chief enemy and paralyzer of the individual will. Habit rules because, as Eddie points out, people are educated not to initiate action. Their chief options are passive expectation or imitation. Imitating one's father, as Walter does, is not really to initiate action: it is merely to respond to a previous pattern. Eddie's discovery that "you could take yourself in hand" is not the old Horatio Alger message of the "self-made man." Rather, it is the assurance that patterns of behavior so strongly habitual that they have become powerful controlling forces can nevertheless be escaped. Eddie preaches the recurring Seager sermon: man can break out; he can be free.

It is not easy to break out, as Walter's degrading odyssey illustrates. The forces eroding the will are staggeringly powerful. Witness the cuckold Walter Herzog, a man made less by the repetition of insult; this, in fact, is the modern condition, a circumstance shown in varying degrees repeatedly throughout the novel. Repetition is the rule, for habit rules Athens: the "habitual deference to the Phelps name," that Walter fails to recognize in the sheriff, counterpoints that official's comment when Walter bails out the drunk Benny Carson, "What in hell you want to get him out for? He'll be right back in?" (191-92). The novel has a number of empty rituals, ceremonies that have deteriorated to mere habit: the fraternity initiation is one, as are the drinking and purchasing of bootleg liquor. The party at the country club hosted by the Iversons captures the sameness of all such parties. When Walter's antisocial behavior transforms the party into a comedy, Mrs. Iverson views it as a disaster, forgetting that she gave the party to cheer up her melancholy husband. He is cheered when Walter disrupts the usual pattern, but habit conquers good intentions, and his wife fails to see that his melancholy has sprung from the very way of life her country club party recapitulates.

The established pattern is indeed very hard to break. The ritual of the Phelpses' evening meal is followed even when they are not hungry; the ceremony is followed religiously even after Todd is killed. It no more occurs to Walter to break the pattern than it occurs to him not to endure the fraternity initiation silliness any longer.

The words "habit" and "custom" recur frequently in *The Inheritance*, and the more outrageous Walter becomes in his defiance of social convention, the more often such words seem to be in his mind. Attempting to "insult" the town with his idleness, Walter nevertheless springs alertly from bed each morning, a leap that "sprung only from habit." He realizes that the hotel clerk's horse betting is not hope, but "habit, sclerotic and monotonous." Walter recognizes the tyranny of habit; he sees it in the townspeople and in himself. But he never seeks the cause. That is left to Eddie Burcham.

When Eddie gains control of his will and performs "the creative act," wishing life for Walter, the implications are multiple. One implication is that the will's freedom to operate lies within the whole man, and as man is fragmented his will is paralyzed. There is no whole man in *The Inheritance*, and Seager deals with that creature more explicitly in *Amos Berry*. But together, Eddie and Walter do constitute the whole man. The old Blakean split of body and soul, head and heart, is to some extent reconciled in the meeting of Eddie and Water at the end of the novel.

A second implication of Eddie's act is the nature of artistic responsibility. Eddie's condition seems to parallel that of the modern artist: dying, outcast from society, he nevertheless thrusts himself upon society and assumes the responsibility of trying to nudge it back onto the path of its salvation; central to that responsibility is the artist's duty to seek out causes and confront the reader with them, no matter how distasteful the causes might be for him. Having displayed the causes, the artist's duty is to suggest remedies. In one sense the novel itself is the remedy: it attempts to revive the atrophied will, and it does so by bucking the tendency of American fiction to "hide" its truths. In *The Inheritance* Seager fulfilled the artistic responsibility he saw was his, and he fulfilled it with an explicitness uncharacteristic of American fiction.

Most reviewers resented the explicitness, perhaps proving D. H. Lawrence's contention in *Studies in Classic American Literature* that "Americans refuse everything explicit." Put off by Seager's explicitness, the reviewers failed even to evaluate his theme. Oddly, they also completely missed Seager's attempt to infuse time into American literature. He was aware that his sense of place was strong, as seemed to be true of most American novelists, and he attempted to counterbalance this with an equally strong sense of time. At most critical instants in *The Inheritance* there are direct references either to time or to timepieces; there are even philosophical discussions of Time's Essence. When Walter is told by his grandmother, "There's more to you than you've ever used before and you'll never get a chance to use it here," she warns that, "There hasn't been anything for a man to do in this town since your grandfather's time except to repeat himself like a clock. Just pile up money" (200–201). Time, in fact, is nearly a character itself. It foreshadows, underscores, and repeats the discovery that both Eddie and Walter make, the discovery that is essential to the revival of the will: "You are living all the time."

The Inheritance met with a lukewarm reception. Yet it is a remarkable novel in many ways; traditional in appearance, it is an attempt to alter the direction of the American novel, specifically with its explicit nature. Its emphasis on time, and its attempts to go beyond the symptoms of a decaying culture to the causes, extended an effort familiar in dealing with the decadent South to the relatively pristine Midwest. *Equinox* and *The Inheritance* are similar in a number of ways, among them the situation of the protagonist at each novel's end. But successful as it was with readers and reviewers, *Equinox*'s more spectacular and unusual form was abandoned for a form resembling that of the nineteenth-century novel. *The Inheritance* marks Seager's shouldering of his artistic responsibility; he had set his own will to work in an attempt to free the paralyzed wills he saw about him.

Chapter Five
Amos Berry

Recalling the Spirit

Amos Berry is Seager's central novel, a position that transcends mere chronology. It is pivotal. *Equinox* and *The Inheritance* were preface and introduction; *Hilda Manning* and *Death of Anger* are epilogue. Seager's first three novels are unmistakably similar. Each proceeds quite logically from its predecessor. But *Amos Berry* represents a conscious readjustment in artistic theory and practice. *Equinox* was occasionally explicit, but fundamentally it was a display of effects, with only vague hints at their causes. The major theme of *The Inheritance* was reiterated frequently, and exploring the personal and historical causes for Walter Phelps's paralyzed will (and, by extension, the general will), Seager is very close, at the end of *The Inheritance*, to the beginning of *Amos Berry*. In fact, Seager declared that he stopped writing *The Inheritance* only when he realized that at some point he had begun writing a different novel entirely. Eddie Burcham's declaration to Walter Phelps, "I think there is more to you than you have ever used" is the border. Here *The Inheritance* leaves off and *Amos Berry* begins.

In *Amos Berry* Seager pinpoints why people have this "more" to them, and he declares his faith in the human spirit. "I think here is where I make my big act of faith but I believe that people are better, have more to them, than the life they have fashioned for themselves can let out," he wrote to Horace Schwartz, editor of *Goad* (June 10, 1953). The finger-pointing in *Equinox* and *The Inheritance* was primarily a passing of judgment. By the time he had finished *Amos Berry*, Seager observed in his letter to Schwartz that he had doubts about the efficacy of such a method: "Now that I have made my gripes, I can say this: I personally am tired of the finger-pointing. Hell, you and I know what the mess is. That is where we live and nobody wants to count over his own chancres. What I would like to see is not even idealistic. It is only the recalling to ourselves of what is already there, the part of us our present way of life will not let us use, in short, the spirit, whatever that means. We have to instal death in the dream so that, knowing the term, life can mean something."[1] Clearly, the dream is the American

Dream; it is a dream of things: material comfort, financial security, material success.

Amos Berry hardly appears to be a potential murderer. At forty-five he seems to be a typical middle-class American. He has a good job, a nice house, and a son in college. He is respected in the small town his forebears helped found. All outward signs indicate that Amos is content. Yet he systematically plots the murder of his employer, Walter Rickert, a man he has known all his life. The murder is orderly, careful, and Amos is never in any danger of being caught. The tension resides in the gradual revelation of Amos's motives, never in a feeling that his arrest may be imminent.

Amos Berry's son Charles narrates and his narrative is an attempt to comprehend his father, a man he greatly misjudged. Charles tries to discover how such a "typical" and apparently "successful" member of the status quo could commit murder, why he would make a Thoreauvian withdrawal to a country farm, as Amos does, rejecting the modern world as completely as he is able. Finally, Charles tries to come to terms with his father's suicide, which obviously is not a result of any feelings of guilt from the murder.

About this relatively simple plot Seager has woven a number of threads: he explores the reasons for Amos's gradually unraveling marriage, examines his tangled relationship with his son, and scrutinizes the job that was steadily strangling the very life out of him. The pattern of Amos's life is common in twentieth-century America, and Seager's ultimate aim is to discover how modern Americans came to be trapped in such a pattern.

A number of American novels, from *Babbit* to *The Man in the Gray Flannel Suit*, have shown the American businessman as either villain or merchant prince. But Seager suggests that American businessmen are, in fact, victims.

Seager lived in automobile country most of his life, but only when he arranged a private tour of the Dearborn Ford plant at the request of a visiting Oxford classmate were his eyes opened to the implications of the assembly line. He saw for the first time the price these men paid for their high wages, and he saw, too, how the business affected not only the workers but a way of life.

Seager took up residence in Tecumseh, Michigan, at a crucial time; he was able to observe the transformation of Tecumseh from a small agricultural community to a small industrial city with a newfound interest in "progress" and development. As Tecumseh Products expanded, Tecumseh changed. However, it wasn't the change that bothered Seager as much as it was the blind faith in the good that "progress" and "development" would bring—as well as the corresponding vague notion townspeople had of these concepts. It wasn't only businessmen who believed that whatever was good for business was good for "people"; after all, Tecumseh products created a number of local millionaires.

To be sure, Seager's sympathetic treatment of businessmen would have been possible without his objective scrutiny of automobile country and a "growing" Tecumseh, but the catalyst was his own compassionate concern for his friends. In a letter to his friend and drinking companion, novelist Earl Karr, Seager cataloged the various illnesses of his businessmen friends. He contrasted them with his father's healthy and vital friends and concluded that they sickened out of boredom. "There are a lot of obvious answers but the one I hold by—and I admit it is an act of faith to do it—is these guys have the battered remnants of some kind of sensitivity stuffed down in the dark retrocaecally, maybe, and they are really bored by what they do."[2] Observing his friends and relatives, as well as his fellow Tecumsehans—for whom he had a bemused affection—Seager discovered that businessmen weren't necessarily the way they were because they wanted to be. They were caught, helpless, in an unavoidable trap.

Seager's first major problem was point of view. How could he best make Amos a sympathetic character while tracing his transformation from an apparently shallow "normal" businessman to a murderer, from a simple representative of the country club set to a complex dropout? Seager considered having Amos keep a diary, then he decided to show Amos through the eyes of his son. "I, the novelist" was a device Seager had considered using with *Equinox*, and he was aware of its inherent weaknesses. To avoid some of the pitfalls, he made the novelist a character in his own story.

Seager makes it clear that Charles Berry is not merely a narrator, that he is, in fact, writing a book—this book. Charles never claims to be writing his father's biography, and he occasionally reminds the reader of the special nature of the narrative he is reading, as when at the end of the scene between his mother and Da Sylva, he adds, "Something like this must have happened."[3]

The Whole Man

Charles Berry's relationship with his father is unsatisfactory until near the end of Amos's life, and only "coincidence" makes it otherwise. The chasm between father and son is predictable, for Seager makes it clear that fathers have little to offer their sons. *The Inheritance* states most strongly that sons are heir only to a meaningless pattern they are doomed to follow, each son becoming merely a diminished version of his father. Charles escapes the pattern by becoming a poet, but in initially escaping the pattern he nearly makes the same mistake Walter Phelps makes. As a poet Charles feels contempt for businessmen, his father included. Charles believes that "his parents lived the way they did because they liked to live that way." His blind contempt, like the blind hatred of Walter Phelps, is merely a block to understanding.

The son cannot escape the influence of his father, whether he accepts it or rebels against it. To do either is to remain in the grip of the same forces that diminished the lives of the fathers. The son must recognize the inheritance that becomes his through his father before he can escape its power, and to recognize the inheritance, he must recognize the father. Only knowledge can disperse illusion. Finding his father, Charles Berry finds himself. One theme of *Amos Berry* is the search for identity, a search carried on by both father and son, for identity is one of the casualties of the forces of impersonality that govern the modern world.

The story of Amos Berry is also the story of Charles Berry. Charles's narrative is an account of the birth of the whole man (there is a death in every creative act, in this case the death of his father), and Charles is this whole man. It is too late for Amos, the stifled visionary whose potential has been smothered. The best he can do, he does: he makes a gift of his vision to the poet with the limited vision. Charles, then, tells his own story as he tells the story of his father.

Charles is complete only when he recognizes himself in his father and his father in himself. Together they make up the whole man. There is something of the poet in Amos, and beneath the protective smugness and the supercilious airs of the poet is some of the human warmth, the natural kindness of Amos Berry. There is little room for doubt, since Seager makes his intentions clear. Charles explains his presence at the murder (a "coincidence" that bothered reviewers, and that they were bothered is an indication of their failure to come to grips with the novel's significance, the very explicitness of its nature). He was at the murder scene because he intended to be there. "It is not the intention that governs talk in the street or shadowboxing or wheedling hospitality out of stupid hosts. It is rather the intention you hope to use in writing poetry, that of the marvelous stranger, the whole man" (222). The whole man? "It is a mystery but one that I believe in," Charles the novelist declares, and in so declaring he echoes Seager's own declaration of "faith."

It is clear that the son is the father's *Doppleganger* even before he announces it. Both father and son deck rivals (Larry Da Sylva and the fraternity man), and in this case the father is assuming an aspect of the son, who took boxing to justify his escape from football. Football is doubtless the best American example of organization as sport, and by escaping football through the individual sport of boxing, Charles anticipated, in a small way, his father's large-scale attempt to flee organization. Amos is also, as Charles points out a few times, a bit of a poet. Amos uses the word "sullen" to describe pines (9), and in a moment of insight, realizing that Judson "who had the true old time grabbiness, the open lechery after money" (169) is the spiritual heir to his own ancestors, the founders of the county, Amos slips into poetic language. " 'He is my father's son. I am free,' he said aloud and he was embarrassed because he had spoken aloud and in a phrase and rhythm like the Testament he had never had time to read even in English" (169).

Amos's discovery that parentage is as much a matter of the spirit as "the blood-lines, the stud-books" only serves to reinforce the idea of the whole man, the merging of the *Dopplegangern*. The reconciliation of father and son is a matter of the spirit. That they are related by blood is only incidental. Charles, as a poet, deals in symbols, and this is how Amos Berry comes to recognize his act of murder, as an act primarily of symbolic value; it would accomplish little "real" good. Charles reinforces the parallel, equating the murder with poetry when he says that like all creative acts, death was essential to the process (225). Isolated, these exchanges, these moments when father and son assume one another's identities, seem almost heavy-handed, but they are subtle enough that no critic or reviewer seems to have caught them. Charles even confesses to his father's crime when Paul Kennedy jokingly accuses him of the murder of Walter Rickert. "To the others he seemed merely tactless but he filled me with terror." And "I found myself asking why, even in joke, I had confessed to my father's crime" (239). The position of Charles's question of his motive in confessing the crime as the last sentence in chapter sixteen is evidence of the emphasis Seager meant it to have. It was, to be sure, intended to be noticed.

Charles struggled against recognizing this other side of himself. The poet in him had to dominate, for the poet had been denigrated those many years before when he declared his intention to become a poet and the Rickerts had laughed and his mother had been silently furious (52). Defiance was essential to survival. So for Charles the process of growing awareness, of recognizing the humanity in his father, is by no means painless, a fact suggested symbolically when Charles, mistaking his own reflection in the mirror for his father's face, drunkenly slugs the mirror and severely gashes his hand (294). But the angry poet does learn some compassion for the businessman and, by extension, for that part of the human spirit that is "forced down into the darkness." Charles makes it clear that early on he had no cause to question his own assumption that "his parents lived the way they did because they liked to live that way" (173). The discovery that he was wrong enables him to see that those he condemned were in fact already condemned; they were victims of forces over which they had no control.

Here is a crucial point, and one that critics of the novel have seemed to overlook: Charles's account is after the fact and from the point of view of a poet, a man who lives "outside the system." The smugness of which one reviewer accuses Charles Berry is in character. Charles is, in fact, quite smug until he "accepts" his father, and a further implication is that only his father's suicide removed the last residue of smugness. If Charles seems smug, it is a measure of his honesty, for as the author-narrator he creates the Charles whom the reader sees. This first-person point of view that Seager's friend, the novelist George Milburn, found so unnecessarily cumbersome is evidence of Seager's artistic good sense. After all, he had things to say, that, had they come from a third-person narrator or an omniscient narrator, would have sounded not only pompous but openly and abrasively didactic. Attention would invariably have been focused not upon the novel, but upon the man behind it. A smug narrator is a small enough price to get away with saying the things Seager said.

"I Wanted It Said"

As he pointed out often enough, Seager had a good deal he wanted to say in *Amos Berry*. He was aware before he began the novel of what he wanted to say, and even before he began to wrestle with the question of how to say it, he discussed "how things got this way" with anyone who had a good mind and a willing ear. He tested his theories, for example, on Roger Burlingame, an author whose specialty was technology, and he tested his historical overview on scholars such as Warner Rice.

Chapter twenty-three rankled reviewers because in it Seager said too much. Charles and Amos engage in a long historical and philosophical discussion in a serious attempt to answer Amos's question, "If I am like the others, how did we get this way?" Seager dared a great deal in this chapter; he was perfectly aware of the modern dictum, "show, don't tell." He was, after all, thoroughly grounded in the history of literature;

he could quote Henry James's advice in the *Prefaces*; he could trace aesthetic theory from Aristotle through Benedetto Croce in Joyce's *Ulysses*. Seager knew what he was getting into when he located the beginning of modern times with Descartes and continued to stalk Western thought through Newton, Locke, the American Revolution, the French Revolution, Adam Smith, Darwin, Sir Charles Lyell, Marx, Freud, and Henry Ford.

The reviews found the dialogue "unlikely" or "unnecessary." Ironically, Seager had "unlikely" conversations similar to this one: with James Goodrich, with Duane Forbush, with George Pollock at Oxford, with a number of young men who wanted to discuss "great concepts" but found their teachers and professors embarrassed at such pretentious talk, preferring instead to deal with technique or individual thinkers. In fact, the difficulty of dealing with "great concepts" was one of Seager's laments. People shied from such talk, ignoring great ideas, the historical forces that shaped their lives: "History is only what I can remember," Amos says, and his death lurks in that sentence.

"I wanted it said, even though I couldn't think of a good novelistic excuse for saying it," Seager said of the father and son dialogue in a letter to novelist Anton Myrer. But the best novelistic excuse of all is implied in his letter; he felt it was his responsibility to include it. He wanted the whole view. "The place to exert your will is in the practice of the craft," as Charles Berry says (142). Thus *Amos Berry* is at once a portrait of Seager's own will and a proclamation: social and artistic.

Seager wanted to change things; he wanted people to live richer lives; ultimately, he wanted to improve the quality of life in America. Making the novel's narrator a poet was no accident, for Seager had a belief in the power of literature that seemed, at times, almost mystical. And why not? Art in the form of literature had demonstrated near-magical powers in his own life. It was refuge and comfort in Memphis. It was an aid to seduction in college. It helped to send him to Oxford, and it secured him a job on *Vanity Fair*, just as it landed him a scripting job that paid for his farm. His literary reputation kept him teaching at Michigan without an advanced degree.

The essence of literature was poetry, and according to James Goodrich, "Allan was always saying—he was certain of it—that eventually a poet was going to come along and straighten things out. He said it so often and so sincerely that at times I believed it myself."[4] The poet was slow in coming, so Seager tried to bring him. Charles Berry, the poet, with his story of his businessman father, became the attempt of Allan Seager to straighten things out.

In the midst of the philosophical dialogue with his father Charles remarks that "There has never been any very good poetry written about science." And when Amos asks if anyone hadn't seen the insidious nature of the "reason as good" approach to life, Charles mentions Blake, Coleridge, and Matthew Arnold. He further declares that Dostoevsky "saw it all." "If it were desired to reduce a man to nothing, it would be necessary only to give his work the character of uselessness." Charles then amplifies Dostoevsky's statement, making it germane to Amos's experience, in one of the many insights with the ring of truth in this novel. "If a man does not know how his functions fit into the whole, doesn't his work have the character of uselessness?" (350). Thus the assembly line worker who assembles one small part again and again, or the office worker who is actually a sheepherder or cattle trader five times removed.

When Amos asks why no one paid attention to Dostoevsky, Charles replies "Dostoevsky was a novelist and people are reluctant to believe that poets and novelists can deal with truth." In fact, poets and novelists are the casualties of the very movement Charles has traced. Reason has triumphed over truth because it is now an article of faith that truth is only a matter of logic, that proper education and proper legislation will eliminate crime. Amos is proof that it won't, for as he notes, he committed murder partly for the reasons he and Charles have discussed—because Rickert was the Organizer—but partly, too, because he was bored.

Masks, Selves, Identities

Amos Berry begins with a juxtaposition of the public Amos Berry and the private one. The face he showed the world was "Office Manager for the Lenawee Corporation," but that wasn't really Amos, it was only a small part of him, and that is at the core of the novel. The real Amos was the thinker, the dreamer behind the mask, the man whom only son and poet had glimpsed: "After the act, the absence, and the death, I can see these odd lapses of my father's as his identifying sign. It pointed to his address, where he really lived" (2). The odd lapses are moments when the mask slips and Amos gazes into the trees or off into the distance, thinking.

Amos "passed for a man who was quietly happy because he had all the materials" (22). Charles understands that this man, the man his mother saw every day, was an actor: "[The stairways] were the wings from which Mr. Amos Berry, concealing a slight nervousness, would soon

emerge for his performance. It was enacted every day and he conscien-
tiously tried to give his audience the interpretation they expected"(26).
Seager's recurring references in this novel to the false appearances that
people assume is no facile portrayal of hypocrisy. Masks (those that
chiefly interest him) are not consciously assumed. Men adopt the faces
expected of them because they have no alternative: their identities are
lost, even to themselves. Impersonal forces create impersonal beings.

Amos arrives at the heart of the matter in his rambling discourse with
Charles at the farm. He points out that charity is organized and impersonal; people perform charitable deeds for people they don't know,
impersonally and from a distance, by writing out a check—not as they
once did, by caring for their neighbors directly. Workers in the soup
cannery don't know the people who will eat the soup; the quality of soup
is no longer maintained by a knowledge that one's friends are eating it
and will judge one's ability to make soup. "The quality of the soup is
maintained, they hope, by standards, and standards are impersonal."
Organization ultimately destroys identity. As Amos puts it, "What are
we losing? Our pride, our self-respect, our very identities. Our selves are
empty" (324).

Amos's heart attack makes him aware of his lost identity, and, aware
of his own public masks, he becomes aware of the public masks of others.
First the doctor, who assumes the white jacket of "famous medical
experts in an advertisement," is seen as more mask than man. He notes
the many masks of Walter Rickert: Napoleon, the Perpetual Businessman, part clown part Brother Maunciple at the cookout. To his wife
Rickert is "a long self-satisfied sheep-like face. A face like a cuspidor, to
spit in." Rickert, who symbolizes for Amos Berry all that is wrong with
the modern world, has no identity—only disguises, for "all the suggestions he gave off merely cancelled out" (60).

Amos's wife, Edith, is determined to act like an English countess with
Da Sylva, but she can only emulate the cliché lovers of the movies. After
the divorce she plays "the chichi New Yorker up to the last curl of her
permanent . . ." (265). The image of "the urban sophisticate," which
is the image she has of herself, would have been "laughably pretentious"
in "our town." To Charles she looks "silly," not because "what she had
jumped at so desperately, an identity, was undignified," but because
"she was too ignorant, too hasty, and worst of all, too late" (284-85).

Numerous minor characters troop across the stage, and the narrator
reminds us from the wings that they, too, are actors: by habit, by the
coercion of circumstance, but actors nonetheless. Major McNabb's ster-
ling interpretation of the perfectly charming English gentleman is

betrayed only now and again by his costume. Marge Rickert plays the desperate alcoholic until Walter's death allows her to abandon the role. Her daughter is an ad, the perfect child.

In Philadelphia Amos recognizes the public masks of public figures: he knows he'll never be able to vote for Dewey because he sees the mask behind the mask when Dewey flashes his three mechanical smiles at the crowd. After his escape to the farm, Amos realizes "with a shock that the standard image of Ford that had lain in his memory beside Washington, Lincoln, and other great Americans had shrunk. He seemed to be now a mean man, wrong and vaguely dangerous" (213). Amos's search for identity is linked to the country's history. Finding his own identity, he begins to see others more clearly for the first time, and those "others" are an ever-widening circle from family to friends to acquaintances to public officials and then historical figures. As so often in Seager's fiction, the first step toward knowledge was self-awareness.

Charles arrives at this self-awareness earlier than his father; having discovered his own masks, he is able to recognize masks on others. This enables him to "find" his father as his father is finding himself. Charles, too, sees the masks of great men, "the faces you see on *Time*, the portrait gallery of the West. If underneath the bone, as I suspect, an unease spurts and dribbles into terror, the fat cheeks hide it, the fat cheeks of power held stiff for the moment of official gravity" (330). Charles's ability to recognize the masks people assume has its rewards. His relationship with Laura will, it is clear, be spared the hypocrisy his parents suffered. Charles recognizes, for example, that Laura's gentleness is not "a mask she had assumed to keep [him] docile," but is in fact her true nature. And he recognizes her "I love you, too, Charles" as an act necessitated by the occasion's demand. This ability is valuable, for distinguishing the "demand of the occasion" from the natural and spontaneous response keeps the two from becoming one. It sounds silly to say that if he were unable to distinguish between the two they would be indistinguishable, but Charles, like his father, has learned the painful commonplace of reality: apprehension repeated becomes as fact.

Masks and roles are the stuff of unity, the artist's instinctive means of imposing order upon a jumble. Seager was not granted his *donné*; consequently, readers and reviewers went looking for a mask when the identity was there before them. None of this "truth safely swaddled in an ark of bulrushes" that D. H. Lawrence saw as characteristic of American literature for Seager. Seager "wanted it said," and it would be absurd to expect a man whose very themes point up the necessity of being explicit to upholster his meaning comfortably until it lay disguised beneath a thick covering of symbol. The mask is a symbol, to be sure (as is the fog that Charles walks in at crucial moments, the same fog that encompasses Amos in his dream), but the symbols are unifying devices and thematic reinforcements; they are never substitutes for theme and meaning. Yet explicit, they went unnoticed; unobtrusive, they function as the best symbols function: they do not get in the way of the novel. But no one noticed this remarkable technical feat.

Man Is Born For Trouble

The novel is an example of the wholeness Seager sought, the wholeness he felt essential to the restoration of the spirit, for in the novel he merges two divergent tendencies of the American novel: the look westward to the frontier and the look eastward to the old culture. It is not the old ways, the old traditions, that Amos wants to destroy, it is what they have become. Rather, Amos seeks to inject the stagnant "manners" of a culture with the old "frontier" energy, thus reviving a dying "spirit." Amos doesn't want to return to the past; he is aware of its deficiencies. Useful work is essential in restoring man's dignity, but, as tombstones attest, "in those days women worked themselves to death" literally. "We can't return to the past," Amos declares (323). But the present desperately needs some of the vitality of the past. Again, a wholeness, a balance, is sought.

Seager attacks the "good life" in *Amos Berry*, and he attacks American optimism, the country's "official" attitude. He was himself the victim of a counterattack by at least one critic, who accused him of blindness to the virtues of America's vitality and optimism, a critic who liked *Amos Berry* very much, but who nonetheless missed a crucial point.[5] For Seager was attacking an empty vitality, an automatic gesture, and a blind optimism.

Seager viewed his own attack as in the best tradition of American literature: "And Emerson popping off, popular, making his single gesture on all the lecture platforms. Optimism, cheerfulness, and the guys who really penetrated, who knew that happiness is a subjective happenstance not a goal in life, not even a possible way to live, and certainly not an 'official' obligation as it is now, who saw that there must be a way to live that includes the immeasurable, the unknown, in fact, the divine, i.e., a moral and spiritual way to live, Hawthorne, Melville, even Twain in his last days, they were ignored partly because of the status of the novel, partly because what they said was unpleasant and did not even seem true."[6] This excerpt from Seager's letter to Horace Schwartz certainly implies that, as an author, Seager was writing in the best company and, well, if he were ignored for many of the same reasons as these three literary giants, it was, in a backhanded way, a justification of sorts.

Amos Berry attempts the heroic, the nearly impossible: to change the ingrained expectation of happiness and substitute that old "bedrock of the culture of the west: Man is born for sorrow as the sparks fly upward." This Amos does for his son Charles.

"I had endured these insults singly, one at a time. They had seemed to come at me in blind lunges, lurching and spinning at random, sheer bad luck. Now, thanks to my father, I could see bad luck had me surrounded. . . . This was how things were and things were bad. When I said this to myself getting dressed . . . I felt a great lightening of the heart as a man who has undergone the lapses into terror and humiliation of fits is soothed when a doctor tells him he has epilepsy and the fits can be expected. When you know the enemy, it is reassuring to take a posture of defense." (353-54)

Knowledge, then, is good no matter how dismal, for it frees one from illusion, and freed from illusion, one can take oneself in hand. It is the cycle Seager found central to James Joyce's stories, and he has put it in American terms: "I wanted to get married at once. If it was going to be tough from now on, I wanted someone with me I could trust, someone beautiful to look at every day. Laura. I had a big feeling of starting out. Maybe it was like that when they left St. Joseph in the wagons going West. I suppose every young guy has to pioneer his country and it's nice to know about dry holes and the bad Indians ahead of time" (354). This is the function Amos has fulfilled, Amos the prophet, warning of the evils in the future, the metaphorical "dry holes and bad Indians." The title Seager wanted for *Amos Berry* was *The Last Pioneer*. Amos may not be the "last" pioneer in the sense of the final pioneer, rather he may simply be the "previous" pioneer, the one who went out just before (in this case just before Charles) and sent word of the dry holes and bad Indians. It is a nice ambiguity, and it is fitting.

Amos Berry ends on a fairly hopeful note. When Charles Berry realizes, thanks to his father, that bad luck has him surrounded and feels "a lightening of the heart," the novel has achieved a satisfying unity. For as Seager suggests, Amos's heart attack is the result of a sick spirit; his heart is betraying him for reasons which, at the novel's outset, he is not even aware. The heart is the obvious traditional symbol, of course, and there are numerous references to it in *Amos Berry*. The implication in this passage is that Charles has escaped the weight on the heart experienced by both his father and his grandfather. Amos, like his namesake the biblical prophet, has attempted an heroic task (the biblical Amos diverts God's judgment) and he has, in a small, personal way succeeded.

Chapter Six
Hilda Manning

I Still Am: A Natural Being

Artistically, *Hilda Manning* was a great success, but the success was entirely personal and private. Allan Seager knew that his fourth novel was very good indeed because "it clicked." Commercially, however, it was a failure. Only five reviews appeared, and sales were minimal. Perhaps because his books had been dogged by such misfortune, Seager looked for someone to blame. He fixed on his publishers, Simon and Schuster, for what he felt was a less-than-adequate publicity campaign, and *Hilda Manning* was the last book he wrote for them.

Whatever the reasons for its commercial failure, *Hilda Manning* certainly justifies Seager's high opinion; it is a superb book. *Hilda Manning* accurately captures, as James Kelly noted, "the brutal sociology of village life."[1] As yet another piece of Seager's Lenawee County, it is an excellent guidebook. Oakville is unmistakably Onsted. One can recognize the old Reynolds place from the description of the Manning farm, just as one can appreciate Seager's description of the Michigan sky after seeing the real thing. Detroit hasn't changed much in the two decades since the novel was written; its sales clerks and automobile workers apparently haven't changed at all. Even the countryside between Onsted and Detroit retains some of the old landmarks: The Rat's Nest, for example, still stands.

Onsted's residents walk the pages of *Hilda Manning*. Seager's aunt, Louella Reynolds, still lives in Onsted, and she can identify the real-life counterparts of most of the characters, including Hilda, Doc Higbee, and Charlie Anslinger. She can point out, as well, the many minute transformations that altered fact to fiction. The coroner's jury, for example, played bridge while the body of the real-life Hilda's husband was being examined. Seager appropriately changed the game to hearts. James Goodrich, another Onsted resident, knows that Sam Larned was to a great extent patterned after him, and he's proud of the fact. Goodrich's mechanical abilities, according to local residents, approach wizardry; he agrees with them. And he will lovingly display his WW II

Luger, to which Seager gave a role in the novel, too. Yet while Seager began writing with the intention of exploring Onsted, and by extension small American villages, through Hilda, Hilda—and not the town—came to dominate.

Hilda Manning is a placid farm wife, so beautiful that virtually all males past the age of puberty lust after her. Her husband, Acel, is appreciably older than Hilda, and as the novel opens, he is mortally ill. Hilda poisons him, perhaps because illness has robbed him of all his dignity, or perhaps because she wants the money and freedom to reclaim her illegitimate son—raised by Hilda's sister Asia as her own. Hilda leaves Oakville and her lover Sam Larned, and when she discovers her son has died, she wanders aimlessly. Eventually she returns home, and though the entire village virtually knows she killed Acel, she is accepted back into the community. She, in turn, accepts Sam Larned, and the novel ends with the promise of marriage and children.

Hilda Manning deals with identity and dignity, just as Seager's first three novels did, but in this novel, the perspective assumed in *Amos Berry* is reversed. Only gradually does Amos become aware of his lost identity and establish (or reestablish) it. From the outset Hilda Manning has no doubts about her own identity; natural female, she is the natural being. Identity and dignity inhere in her, the one assuring the other. She exists, and in her existence there is none of the Cartesian separation of mind and body. Hilda echoes Descartes's "Cogito Ergo Sum" with her "I still am."[2] But in her statement there is no compartmentalization. She "still is" physically; for Hilda existence simply is, and thought is merely one of its aspects.

Exemplifying an unfragmented, natural existence, Hilda, throughout the novel, is identified with nature by the novel's characters and by its narrator. She moves "gracefully as a cat" (34), she doesn't squint her eyes in sudden light as people normally do (59), and she has eyes "like a cat's" (116). Sam notes that "her eyes were like hawk's eyes" (198). Acel compares her to fire: "It was never a question of satisfaction when it's like you're feeding a fire, blowing and turning in a night wind. . . . It might light and warm you but you know the fire didn't care" (115).

Hilda has an almost unnatural ability to raise animals (she saves young pigs with the unheard-of-feat of teaching them to drink milk from a saucer), she seems to understand them and to communicate with them (the raccoon in the ridgerunners' apartment in Detroit), but it is with water, never with fire, that she identifies herself. The identification with water (functioning as the traditional life symbol as well as the "natural") runs throughout the novel. "A man coming at her would have said she was thinking, dreaming, kind of, but the grace and quiet was not dream. She was watching the late-summer haze hanging blue against the woods and to watch it was as much a day's event as eating" (51). And:

Watching the haze patiently, delightedly until she could see its movement, slow, indolent and stately, she was aware of it as water lifting. No one had told her of the veins of water in the ground issuing as springs to feed the rivers, lakes and ponds, but she knew them as well as she knew the flow and play that went on inside her hand, the silent pools seeping upward grain over grain, little stone over little stone, blocked and seeping around rocks, then stones and grains of earth until enough had risen to make the swamp or the spring in the woods; or the near ones, not deep down, already found by roots, tendrils fine as hair, the soundless, slow, blind reaching, the wet success. If she let herself she could see a clump of grass as a green fountain. The aqueous veining of flower petals enchanted her as much as their color, and a tree was like a father, strong to force his way down in secrecy and darkness to the prime. (52)

Hilda, unable to swim, "envied the fish because they lived there, drinking their solid and transparent air where she herself was bound irrevocably to cups and glasses and bottles and palmsful from springs they had bullied into the house through pipes metal and unnatural" (52). Hilda's bath is "a renewal, not thought of, led to it by a custom of the nerves, and not a ritual to clean off any shame" (52).

Hilda watches the rain impassively as Sam tries desperately to impress her with his remodeling efforts done only for her, and Sam mistakenly interprets her attention to the rain as the concern of a farmer's wife (90). When Hilda's labor pains start, she goes to the pump for water while Asia runs off to get a doctor, and though she can carry only a small amount, carry it she must (108). The numerous references to water are often suggestive of Hilda's state. As she flees Oakville, for example, the references to water become more scarce and, for Hilda, less satisfying. The Mississippi disappoints her. The old, dirty snow depresses her. As she closes in on her decision to return to Oakville, snow comforts her; she stands by the window, "watching the destruction of the city by the fresh snow" (285). In the museum with Donald she moves straight to the fountain (274), and of course she offers water to the suddenly ownerless raccoon (like her a wild creature caged in the city) in the "apartment of the ridgerunners" (290).

But Hilda's flight is directed by water. She goes to Detroit because "when you are rich you live in a city. It could have been any city, New

York, San Francisco, New Orleans, on their different waters" (257). Hilda's mind can conceive only of cities "on their different waters," no landlocked cities.

"A Tree with Eyes"

Seager makes extensive use of water in *Hilda Manning*, but more extensive is his symbolic use of trees. There are over one hundred separate allusions to trees in *Hilda Manning*. They are never intrusive, but they are always there; they don't interfere with story or theme, but they do offer another level of meaning for those who choose to explore it. Seager was aware of the long history of the tree as a symbol of the affirmation of life; in his Yeats-Joyce class he expressed admiration for Yeats's use of the tree in his poetry.

Trees appear throughout the body of Seager's work, early and late, and they appear at crucial moments: the maples in "This Town and Salamanca" reinforce that story's theme, and nearly thirty years later, Amos Berry stares at the maples when he is in his private world; these are the moments by which his son identifies him. But in no work are trees more numerous than in *Hilda Manning*.

The tree is no subconscious symbol in this novel (although its extensive use may well be). Seager's working title for the novel was "A Tree with Eyes" (Acel says, "Even before I marrried her, when she looked at me it was like a tree with eyes and it still is. . . . " (116), but in considering himself notoriously bad with titles, Seager acquiesced at once to his agent's rejection of that title. Nevertheless, his intention is evident in his own first choice.

Trees were important to Seager, though he was never explicit about the reasons for their importance. In his notes, near the end of his life, he asked, "Why do I live here, ten miles from my birthplace?" One of the answers was, "When I read that Claude Rains, English-born, died in Franconia N.H. it seemed a shame. He should have died in England. Why here? It may just be the trees, to look out of a window and see the trees of my childhood."[3] Sam Larned echoes these thoughts: "It was the trees that kept him there, the maples and the elms that overarched the street to where the stores began, the maples and the pear tree in the yard when he was a boy, the shagbark hickories beside the roads, and the walnuts, oaks and maples in the woods . . . and if he could have recalled the candor he had used with his mother when he was a little boy he would have said right out, 'The trees.'" The rest of the passage makes the connection between trees and Hilda: "People he could defy all right, affront, insult them as he knew he might have to do, but you cannot defy a tree. It is there. It keeps pace with time, changing, green and bare, but it is not in time, not your time, anyhow, what you do beneath it passing and repassing, makes a difference, or he believed it did" (19).

As George Hunt realizes, Hilda is a witness. When men do something in front of her, her presence "makes a difference," makes their acts real (Hunt's observation adds another dimension to Acel's "a tree with eyes"). And later Hilda's serene nature is explained in a paragraph that is reminiscent of Sam's thoughts on trees and time:

The past had been mere fact, all its alternatives stifled by its happening, worthless like the future, a jelly of impossibilities, impossible to calculate because there were so many. As she was sensual enough to do it she had lived in the brief adventitious ecstasies of the moment, confident, since one season followed another, that the supply would never fail. . . . It was enough to yearn, and, almost nobly imperturbable, she had taken things as they came. You could not, she believed, command or manage any more than you could interrupt bird flight or leaf change. This had given her serenity. Until now. (129)

The trees in *Hilda Manning* are the best kind of symbol, infinitely suggestive, pointing to an area of feeling that can neither be made completely explicit nor categorized. Trees are linked to the triumph of life over death, to the seeking of water—life's very source—to a sense of place, to dignity, to the natural, to a sense of time, to a plethora of interrelated concepts. Somehow trees suggest all the good things that modern man has lost. A tree, like Hilda, "is there," and its very quality of "thereness" cannot be defied.

Hilda's movement "had the instant propriety of a tree giving before the wind." Hilda stations herself with trees when she rejects men's work as a silly "custom," making it clear that her own "work" is a "secret joke," a "mocking imitation of [men's] solemnity," and asks the rhetorical question, "What work does a tree do?" It can hardly be coincidence that Hilda kills Acel immediately after verifying that "her woods" are being cut down, woods that Acel has sold for timber. "They were really cutting down her trees. Far down the lane she saw Acel walking toward the house. She left the window and went to the kitchen cupboard. When she shook the stuff into the coffeepot, her hand was steady" (151).

The true horror in killing Acel lay simply in the disruption of nature. For the first time in her life she considered changing events rather than accepting them, living in them with her usual serenity. Thus, as with the water, trees become more scarce as Hilda flees and moves toward

Nebraska. And when Hilda decides to confess her murder to Donald Simms, "then maybe everything would be all right, green trees and smiles. . . . " (285). When she decides at last to walk down the main street of Oakville in the open, the trees are again her witness: "The houses and the trees began" (296).

Revealing to Hilda that she has been cleared of Acel's murder, George Hunt thinks of her as a doe in the woods (301): the trees are indeed back again. A few moments earlier Hunt had thought, "What ever happens here? Our cows are tame. Our horses sold off. They ain't anything wild but pheasant in those woods and Charlie Anslinger's cutting them down one tree at a time" (300). Here is another intersection of the numerous implications of trees. Hilda is something wild and natural, the doe in the woods, and Anslinger is cutting down the trees. His destruction of the trees touches off Acel's murder. At the same time, the trees suggest home and a sense of place: returned at last to the familiar, to home, "the trees began" for Hilda.

In the final three sentences of the novel, after Hilda has asked Sam to marry her, trees are there in a last invocation of the triumph of life, of existence, of Hilda's declaration, "I still am." "The air was fresh and through the bare limbs of the maples the sky was bright with long veils and eddies of stars. It would soon be spring and all the ceremonies would begin again. She hoped all her children would be boys" (312). Through the limbs of the familiar maples Hilda sees not a hope for the future, but merely a fact of nature. Spring will return, and the trees and life will flourish once again. It is merely life's pattern. Hope is indeed a small part of what will be. She will have children; she hopes they will be boys, and the nature of hope is suggested in the echo of Hilda's earlier whimsical view: it would be entertaining to watch men through the whole cycle of growth.

Hilda watches trees as another might tell beads. In this novel, ultimately, trees are "there," just as Hilda is "there." And this "thereness" is something that men have lost, that they need to regain, and that, in desiring to possess Hilda Manning, the men in the novel are attempting to reacquire. "I still am," is an affirmation of life, of "thereness," a witness to the present.

Identity and Dignity

Perhaps Hilda's natural dignity is a by-product of an identity that is still intact. Hilda's identification is with existence, with life itself, and her brief crisis comes when she violates her own devotion to the natural

stream of life's events and hastens Acel's death. Her act, with its
possibility of money as a secondary motive, parallels Acel's decision to
cut down his woods for money. Both acts subvert the natural order of
events; death's season arrives artificially, and both acts are at least
partially motivated by the desire for material gain. However, Acel's act
is a symptom of his disease, his lost dignity. Hilda's act becomes a cause
of her own brief loss of dignity. The murder of Acel also touches the
question of identity. Hilda wishes to be something she cannot be as long
as Acel is alive: she visualizes herself as "mother."

Dignity is eroded in numerous ways. One is illness. From the first
Seager story, "The Street," to his last works of fiction collected in *A
Frieze of Girls*, dignity is eroded by serious illness. Often, as in *Amos
Berry* and *The Inheritance*, disease is viewed as a symptom of general
societal ills. The connection is made in *Hilda Manning* by Doc Higbee.
"Despair and bitterness and anger did not lodge only in the memory.
They blossomed elsewhere in other, almost chosen soils, the heart,
the lungs, the stomach or the vascular system, and gnawed at them,
demolished them in their peculiar ways" (67). Acel's heart trouble
breeds fear, and the fear makes it impossible for him to do his "proper
work," farming (69). Unable to do his proper work, his dignity is eroded
and he develops cancer. It begins, as so often in Seager, with "heart"
trouble (while Acel is dissected, the jury plays "Hearts").

Hilda knows that "work" is merely a created means of identifying
oneself, and her knowledge is central to Seager's theory of what has gone
wrong. People identify themselves by what they do, which is fine if their
work is inherently meaningful or dignified. As he suggested in *Amos
Berry*, Seager believed that farming and the arts were among the last
bastions of dignity in the twentieth century. An exchange between Acel
and Hilda exemplifies his theory well:

> "From next Monday on, I'm a peddler. I'm not a farmer any more."
> "You're Acel Manning, no matter what you do."
> She was cutting up the meat on her plate and she did not see him stare at her
> or how angry and uncomprehending the stare was. A man was nothing without
> his proper work. (135)

Hilda finds her identity simply in survival. Rather than personified
passivity or automatism, as some reviewers seemed to see her, she is the
rare being who has not suffered a dissociation of mind and body—flesh
and spirit, heart and head, or any of these Blakean pairs. The decision is

made for Hilda on an instinctual level, for her identification is with life. Not so the other characters.

The men attracted to Hilda see in her a means of identifying themselves and, therefore, a means of gaining dignity. His dignity in danger because of the illness that has softened him, Acel needs Hilda more than ever before. His "What do you think of me, Hilda?" and "Ever dream about me at night?" are attempts to establish his identity through her. Like Acel and Fenton, Sam suffers an erosion of self through fear. Hilda is his only means of counteracting the fear. "It had relieved him when she spoke and used his name, for he was afraid he was anybody" (54). Donald Simms follows Hilda in a grand romantic gesture in contrast to his dull, pointless existence. "Where do I come in? What am I?" he asks Hilda.

In Detroit dignity is generally nonexistent. It is harder to be someone, to find one's proper work, in the city than in the country. The ridge-runners in Hilda's apartment are representatives of characters that recur in Seager's work: the Southerners who have abandoned their proper work (and their freedom and dignity) to come to a big city and make money. Americans habitually confused appearance and dignity, Seager felt. The poor, persons in certain occupations—waiters, janitors—were automatically thought to lack dignity. Asia represents this confusion of reputation, appearance, with dignity. She has misinterpreted the dignity her grandfather possessed, channeled it into the modern concern for "reputation," "what will people think?" (Of her drunken father? of the family? of Hilda's by-blow? of the beer visible in the grocery sack?)

For all its shortcomings the small village offers a possibility of dignity. There are Hilda, after all, and George Hunt. And, as a final confirmation, Seager has offered the reader the coroner's jury. They act in defiance of the usual village standard of "What will people think?" At the same time, they recognize the dead Acel's right to dignity, and they refuse to accuse Acel of suicide in order to justify their own desire to save Hilda: "*Death by arsenic poisoning. Manner of ingestion unknown*" (256).

Perhaps a metaphor is at work here. The message that was so explicit in *Amos Berry* is suggested in this novel by the relationship between Hilda and her men: for mankind to regain some of its lost dignity (Acel), for mankind to reassume its lost identity (Donald Simms and his fabricated tales), in fact, for mankind to avoid self-destruction (Sam Larned and his suicidal memories, destruction rooted in the past), it must adapt once again to the natural order (Hilda).

Of course, at odds with his belief that things desperately needed changing was Seager's determinist streak. That ever-present tandem in

Seager's works, escape and acceptance, complicates things considerably. But then, one of Seager's few ventures into simplification was the opinion that simplification was too often falsification. So *Hilda Manning* marks yet another unsuccessful flight for a Seager character. Hilda's "flight" from Oakville to assume motherhood is first an attempt to take events into her own hands. It becomes an effort to escape when she learns her son is dead. However, only her return holds any promise of expiation, as she learns. In fact, and this is a major difference from Seager's other novels, her return is a resumption of the natural order, and in this case an acceptably dignified existence. Return brings with it the promise of spring and "all the great ceremonies," the renewal of life, children. Clearly, the struggle for survival is often its own reward in the Seager view: obviously, the pioneers struggling to survive existed with more dignity than the Amos Berrys and Walter Phelpses, who nearly drown in the leisure time they struggle with. Hilda Manning is survival, but she is also acceptance. At odds on one level (the acceptance of a life without dignity and a self that is no self), the two are complementary on another.

The Rewards of Acceptance

Hilda exemplifies the hope in acceptance. Consequently, *Hilda Manning* offers more hope than Seager's other novels. One aspect of this paradoxical nature of acceptance is suggested by Doc Higbee:

These people believe they are blessed, protected, immortal. A European would howl and complain; war, sickness, debt, and death are too common on his anthill. To pretend they did not exist would make him a fool to himself and to others. Why can't we admit these things exist? People sicken and die here also but the sickness and the deaths are not passionately recognized. We try to ignore them as interruptions of a theoretical felicity. Was it the Jefferson twisters? (124)

Higbee's thoughts echo those expressed by Seager in his letter to Horace Schwartz: "We have to instal death in the dream so that, knowing the term, the life can mean something." Hilda accepts death; she also installs it in the dream.

Again, Seager repeated often that Thomas Jefferson was very wise to promise not happiness but its pursuit. Identity and dignity are to be found in the struggle, not in its fruits. Higbee's thoughts on the subject lead to his marvelous parable of the exotic ocean fish who live in eternal gloom, "each living by its own small light." The gloom ("Man is born for darkness as the sparks fly upward") is the fish's natural, unquestioned environment. He accepts gloom and survives by his own small light. "They also live on the past, a certain percentage of interest, so to speak, from an earlier time" (126-27). The Higbee parable, which leaves Hilda "rapt," suggests existence as it is, as Europeans accept it. Americans unrealistically refuse to accept the gloom, and for this they suffer unnecessarily.

"It was only a long time ago that nice things happened," Asia thinks. And her attitude toward the childhood she and Hilda shared illustrates the narrator's point. Asia lives under the delusion that she can escape the gloom of the present by means of a Chevrolet franchise for her husband, thus assuring a deepening of the gloom when the franchise fails to bring the expected happiness and freedom from worry. Miss McIntyre seeks to break out, to escape from the past that has held her captive. She experiences a brief exhilaration when she makes the grandly romantic decision to break with her past and sell her house and belongings. But, in fact, her existence changes almost unnoticeably.

Acel experiences this brief exhilaration, this false sense of breaking out (again, the illusion of escaping the past and altering the present for the better), when he counters the "inculcated frugality of his upbringing" to buy Hilda a diamond (36). His pleasure is shortlived, and his hope that this "big magic" will alter the present is soon shattered. Sam, Donald Simms, and the prostitute in Toledo who longs for culture, "only trying to be somebody she not quite was" (231), all of these illustrate in varying degrees the same evasion.

Hilda, "quiet and receptive as a flower," best demonstrates the rewards of acceptance: "almost nobly imperterbable, she had taken things as they came" (128-29), but she is not the only one. George Hunt has a fierce dignity and a command of his life. He is a rare—in this novel—male realist. The other example is Charlie Anslinger, who marries the marvelous talker, Ollie Maxwell. "After several years of what seemed to be sulking, Charlie had taken to listening, not to what she said at all, but to the monstrous vitality of her saying it until he developed a queer pride, gladly introducing her to strangers and summer people and then standing back to hear her perform as if she were a unique celebrity like Annie Oakley—which, of course, she was." Anslinger's situation is not unlike Seager's relationship with "the people he grew up among." He sulked and was irritated by them at first. And as he accepted them for what they were (their vitality and his origins at the same time), he began to show them off in his fiction. The letters he wrote during the last decade of his life demonstrate again and again an honest delight in the antics of his small-town neighbors.

The hope that *Hilda Manning* offers through acceptance may have had its roots in Seager's personal situation as he wrote the novel. He had "said it all" in *Amos Berry* and his all had not been rejected so much as ignored. His wife's health was deteriorating more rapidly, her disabilities were becoming more obvious, and her healthy periods less frequent. He was depressed. More than ever, his lifelong doctrine of acceptance needed reinforcement. Since the outside held little promise of reinforcement, restoration had to come from within, and it came in the form of *Hilda Manning*. No previous protagonist of a Seager novel had made it all the way through to the other side. Richard Miles and Walter Phelps appear to have seen the light. Amos Berry can only offer hope to those who follow after him. But Sam and Hilda have triumphed, albeit quietly. Spring and children are certain; acceptance is rewarded.

Chapter Seven
Death of Anger
The Implications of Despair

Allan Seager's most hopeful novel, *Hilda Manning*, was followed in 1960 by his most desperate, *Death of Anger*. His wife's hopeless condition moved him to contemplate the darker, more threatening side of his philosophy. For a brief time Seager considered the possibility that the individual will was helpless. Contemplating "having" to support his father and "having to stick by Barbara," he remarked in his notes, "These two situations consumed a lot of my energy but the subjective feeling I have is that they were not of my making, that I had no choice, no other courses open to me."[1] Seager did as he had always done; he dragged out his dim perceptions and, in the cold light of his fiction, illuminated the menace lurking within. Despairing, he faced the most ominous implications of his despair.

Hugh Canning is truly trapped in *Death of Anger*. He is a wealthy American businessman who marries a woman because of her beauty; she marries him because of her father's injunction to find a good provider. Both are shortsighted and too naive to realize, until too late, that Hedwig is a lesbian. Hedwig takes to her bed in despair and shock after their wedding night and remains there, self-invalided, for twelve years. Canning is too concerned with appearances to take action of any sort. In fact, he hopes at first that things can change, that he can someday have a normal marriage and children. Eventually he seeks a spiritual heir, of sorts, to take over his business empire. But Donald, the young man he chooses, rejects his offers and rejects Hugh Canning and all that he stands for as well. When Canning falls in love with Hedwig's nurse, Flora, he takes her to France, fully intending never to return to Hedwig or to his business.

Flora, however, is not the innocent Canning has believed her to be, and eventually he discovers that he has a rival from home, Donald. When Donald is killed in an automobile accident, Canning loses Flora—the only purpose and direction his life has had—permanently. He contemplates suicide, but rejects it for no apparent reason and returns to life with Hedwig. In his absence Hedwig has discovered a purpose: she makes a career of entertaining and dominating her social inferiors. The novel ends ironically, with Hugh Canning, spiritually dead, the envy of the town.

The last two sentences of *Death of Anger* are chillingly hopeless: "But as a matter of fact I am like a man living in the desert. I go to the water hole every day, not that I like water, or that it sustains life, only that I go to the water hole every day."[2] Thus Canning, the novel's protagonist, describes his defeat. "Man is born for sorrow as the sparks fly upward," the restorative which Seager's first four novels prescribed for Western civilization (if a poison, a counterpoison; if an irritant, a counterirritant as well) seems in *Death of Anger* to have become a fatal diagnosis rather than a possible cure, for the novel contains none of the hope implicit in Seager's other novels, the hope that at once represented his innate romantic streak and served as his declaration of faith in the human spirit and the human will.

It is clear that unreined despair can imprison the will as effectively as unreined optimism. Flight is no corrective for either optimism or despair, for both are subjective conditions. Thus the limited options Hugh Canning feels at the end of *Death of Anger* are of his own creation, and though *Death of Anger* holds out no hope for the protagonist, it does reaffirm a number of precepts from Seager's first four novels: one cannot own people; one's responsibility must, ultimately, be to individuals rather than to groups; freedom comes from within; one does not escape the forces opposing the will's action through flight.

Canning is a variant of the earliest Seager protagonist, the man who "breaks out," a direct descendant of "This Town and Salamanca"'s John Baldwin. Canning says at the end of *Death of Anger*, "They admired *me*, nosing at me, asking me as if there were a recipe. These were the voices of their secret lives, the really serious occupation, the daydream they kid about" (213). While John Baldwin defied the conventions that kept residents of "this town" trapped, Hugh Canning only seems to have lived the dream of those who admire him. They admire an illusion, consequently their dreams lack possibility. The narrator of "This Town and Salamanca" arrives at a stage of greater awareness; he knows that his dreams have remained dreams while John Baldwin made his dreams real. In *Death of Anger* there is not even the glimmer of hope that accompanies the coming to awareness, the glimmer that holds the possibility of change. Rather the "secret lives, the really serious occupation" of Canning's admirers is directed toward mere illusion, for Canning has not escaped. The dream is a dead one. This irony is a harsh presentation of the warning that runs throughout Seager's fiction: "Live your dream or lose it." In *Death of Anger* a darker implication lurks within the warning—the life people fashion for themselves gives birth to trivial dreams, dreams hardly worth living.

First, a Seager protagonist has to gain some insight into his own situation, to assess reality. Then he can begin the process of "breaking out," whatever that entails. John Baldwin breaks out of "this town." Richard Miles breaks out of his passive acquiescence to forces smothering his will. Walter Phelps breaks out of the meaningless pattern of existence thrust upon him by his environment and his personal inheritance. Amos Berry breaks out of his "act" and into his "real life," and in so doing, he enables his son Charles to break out as well. Hugh Canning is merely another variation in a long series of Seager protagonists; he differs in that he fails absolutely and completely.

The key to his failure is specified by the novel's title. Again and again the need for strong emotion is suggested, and Hugh can't come up with it at crucial moments, as when Donald shows up in France. He would rather keep the surface smooth, keep the illusion of smoothness intact. The prevalence of blows in Seager's fiction underscores the need for strong emotion—Todd Phelps hits his neighbor and gains great satisfaction, Walter Phelps exorcises his father's ghost by hitting his Uncle Eri, Charles Berry decks the frat man and smashes his own reflection in a mirror—but Canning can only strike a feeble blow to the side of Flora's head, too little and too late. Canning's anger dissipates; he has lost the ability to be genuinely angry. So, despite his symbolic blow to the whole female "tribe" at whose hands he has suffered enough, Hugh's triumph is fleeting. He is, as he suggests, emotionally dead.

If any will is active at the novel's end, it is Hedwig's. Hedwig survives simply on a desire for revenge, reinforcing the suggestion that strong emotion is necessary for the will's survival. In fact, Hedwig's situation often counterpoints Hugh's. Her disillusionment is certainly as shattering as his own, and her coming to awareness is as painful. She is a victim of her own innocence and ignorance. She has seen only the conventional, and she tries to play the required role. Innocently, she believes that she is the only creature of her kind, like the phoenix. She is not attracted to men; she marries Hugh because of convention—her father's advice to marry a good provider—just as Hugh hopes to change her via convention, giving her the new house that every woman wants (51). Hedwig takes to her bed rather than continue the impossible role of normal woman, and even as she lashes out at Hugh she is looking outside herself for a pattern of behavior—she apes television. Hedwig's eventual triumph may be petty. It is easy to belittle the significance of her will's action. Nevertheless, Hedwig is clearly alive. In this she surely has avenged herself on Hugh Canning.

A Difficult Task: Narrator and Structure

Although *Death of Anger* displays the recurrent Seager motifs, it is not as satisfying as Seager's other novels, and its lack lies only incidentally in Canning's despair. That Seager's major theme could be effectively presented with a negative example can hardly be denied. Obviously any failure, from an auto accident to a failed omelette, can suggest a positive theme: drive carefully, cook carefully. The novel's weakness is not in the negative presentation of its theme; rather it is in the protagonist himself. Seager set himself a difficult task when he made Canning narrator, for in Canning he had to combine myopia and keen perception and make the combination believable. He nearly succeeded, and if he had not felt compelled to entrap Canning in futility and despair with such finality, Seager might have triumphed.

Canning has discovered so much about the forces restraining him, he has gained so much knowledge and exhibits so much insight that his complete surrender doesn't quite ring true. As he begins his "therapy"— the written investigation of his own situation—Canning declares that the triviality of life has to do with trivial desires: "Fear and laziness temper our desires. We get tame, I guess, and modestly wish for moderate rewards" (30). And though he acknowledges the central role that chance and circumstance play, Canning knows the individual ultimately controls his own life: "As nearly as I can be honest, I think I must take blame for the results of my actions, regardless of the hopes they were begun with" (30). Canning is simply too intelligent, aware as he is of the paradox implied in his fate:

"I am a free agent. It is the tradition of the country, one of the amiable legends that makes, no matter how pocked and chipped it grows every day, our opinion of ourselves. We all like to think we could borrow an axe, take twenty-eight dollars, dive into a nearby woodlot if such there be, and come out a year later, bronzed and healthy, with a sack of beans to trade. This is nonsense but I didn't know it then." (36−37)

Canning knows he is a free agent, and he knows just as certainly that he is not free. Convention, habit, the accidents of a lifetime all conspire to limit his freedom. It is easy to believe that Hugh Canning could enter into his relationship with Flora blindly, ignoring the "lessons of a lifetime." But it is not easy to accept the fact that having struggled to learn the lay of the land, the bad Indians, and the waterholes, having paid so heavily for his knowledge, he would give up so completely.

This is not to say that Seager failed in either his characterization of Hugh Canning or in the book itself. The degree to which he succeeded is a tribute to his skill, for he set himself a very difficult task. First, Canning himself is charged with the investigation into his own complex failure, an investigation that encompasses many levels: psychological, personal, social, and historical. The investigation and the implications of the investigation are revealed by Canning and in Canning's own words. The third-person point of view would no doubt have provided greater opportunities for displays of wit and irony, as would the first person had the narrator been Donald or Monkey Frazer. These things Seager sacrificed, just as he sacrificed his usual emphasis on things, on the numerous physical details which typify his first four novels. He lost such a great deal by making Canning the narrator that what he hoped to gain takes on a good deal of significance, and what he stood to gain must certainly have been the hope that he could effectively demonstrate the American illusion of "success." It is as if he had decided to make Walter Rickert, with all his limitations, narrator and protagonist of *Amos Berry*. Seager must have understood the risk, the impact he was sacrificing. Amos's reckless act had an inherent enormity; Hugh's flight with a young woman seems diminutive by contrast. And it is in this contrast that Seager's problem is most obvious: he had to infuse Canning's little act with the enormous implications underpinning it, implications as dramatic and consequential as those motivating Amos's act of murder.

With careful structuring he managed to bring it off quite well. Generally, Hugh Canning's sudden lapses into naiveté do not jolt the reader because the reader's path has been carefully and subtly smoothed for him. One device smoothing the way is Seager's careful manipulation of chronology. Hugh approaches his present condition obliquely, only gradually revealing the true sequence of events and the true nature of his problems. Thus the early, truly naive Hugh Canning serves as a convenient cover for the later, more sophisticated one. That is to say, the reader is often cognizant of the two Hugh Cannings—the naive and the knowledgeable—so it is not quite as bothersome as it might otherwise have been when Canning the narrator steps out of character and apes his earlier self, as with "that fellow Dufy's pictures" (196).

The carefully managed chronology not only effectively unfolds the tale itself, but it also provides Seager with the opportunity to gradually expand the implications of Canning's failed life without seeming too obvious. The complex tangle of events and circumstances governing Hugh Canning's life is made quite plausible—almost simple, it seems at times—by a careful unraveling. Events and situations call up like events and situations, actions are foreshadowed, and even before those actions are disclosed Canning has presented possible motives. The foreshadowings and transitions in *Death of Anger* are among Seager's best, and the shifts in time make them especially effective.

The present brackets *Death of Anger*, and everything within the brackets serves to illuminate this present. The question "How did things get this way?" is ever in the background. In fact, chapter one contains the rest of the novel much as a leaf contains not only the seed which once contained it but the history of the tree which grew from the seed. Hugh Canning searches through his environment and his own past, root and branch, seeking the forces, the half-visible causes, that have led him to the hopeless situation in which he finds himself as the novel opens. The first chapter reveals that his existence is pretty bleak. He does business only because "You have to have something to do," and he reveals that he has attempted the escape all businessmen dream of, giving the lie to the dream. All this is couched in wry humor, interspersed with the antics of drunken Johnny and the laughable Old Frank, so that the truly desperate nature of Canning's day-to-day existence is made completely clear only when he returns to the present in the last chapter with his utterly dismal final words.

Chapter one foreshadows what Hugh only gradually reveals. Johnny, who drinks because he hasn't anything to do, is like "the mule who ran full tilt into the side of a barn not because he was blind but because he didn't give a damn" (6). The "story of the mule" within the story of Johnny within the story of Hugh Canning suggests the form of the novel: all its parts tell the same story; the accumulation gives it its force. In fact, Hugh reveals that Old Frank is the catalyst that has triggered his own comprehension:

"I had done, you see, what he was only talking about. I had chucked everything and gone away with a girl. Gone away and come back, and since my arrival, I had been stumbling around like a guy after an auto wreck, in shock, vaguely wondering what had happened to me. Old Frank had told me, as far as one person can tell another anything. I would not have known this as soon, maybe I would never have known it, if I hadn't come to the fraternity reunion to do a little chrome business with Frank, and if I hadn't found this out I don't believe I would have started to write all this down."(14)

Hugh begins his search through his own past with "Maybe it will be a therapeutic activity [to write it all down]" (14). That last chapter, the final return to the present, counterpoints chapter one quite effectively. The hopelessness couched in wry humor in chapter one is stripped bare in · chapter fourteen. Hugh can see the irony of his situation—admired by other husbands, having done what they only dream about—but the irony is bitter. Thus the novel's end gains its sense of hopeless finality from its very beginning, for even the therapy has failed. In fact, the effect of writing it all down has been quite the opposite of therapeutic; it has ensured the triumph of the disease.

The novel's time shifts are carefully ordered. There is, in fact, a symmetry to their arrangement that, nonetheless, seems natural—the proper order for Canning's thought to take. From the present in chapter one Canning gradually works backwards in time, one event suggesting its progenitor in an earlier event. Hugh works his way back until he finds what he thinks is missing, then he moves toward the present once again. However, he never gets beyond the boundary of his own life, suggesting Amos Berry's limitation: "History is only what I can remember." The first half of the novel works from present to past and back to the present again. Hugh tags each foray into the past with its date, so that the time shifts are never confusing, and if he occasionally prefaces an event with commentary from the present it serves to reinforce the structure, for it reminds the reader that the entire novel is a commentary from the present's vantage point.

Canning remains strictly within the realm of the immediate past for the last half of the novel, with the exception of chapter eight, the events of April 1958 (incorrectly dated 1957), the beginning of his affair with Flora Killian. Canning plunges back into his childhood, 1922, after which his account progresses chronologically through the spring and summer of 1958 to his October return—the dying season—and the present moment.

The first half of *Death of Anger* is basically preparation—perspective— for the more recent events chronicled in the last half. The form of the whole reflects Canning's method. Characteristically, he arrives at climactic moments gradually; his chronicle sidles up to important moments, approaching them obliquely. Thus the reader learns early in chapter two that Hugh has a wife who is not "understandable," but Canning must move through his return from the war, the origins of his attraction to Hedwig, the nature of his relationship with women from his college days onward, then edge back toward the present with the arrival of the Finns in his part of the country, the war, and his courtship, before he can reveal, in chapter three, the disastrous wedding night. After that, Canning begins his gradual movement toward the next bit of essential information, that Hedwig is a lesbian. Then he can introduce another essential character in his narrative, Donald. Canning backs off momentarily, working the past for a few more necessary nuggets, and then in chapter eight, at the center of the novel, he cautiously slips in the last major figure, Flora Killian.

Canning is a businessman; it is a fate he cannot escape. Seager makes the method of Canning's narrative consistent with his businessman's nature. Canning abhors loose ends: even as he prepares to take flight from his business, despite the fact that he does not really intend to return, and despite the fact that he "didn't particularly care" what happened during his absence, Canning carefully anticipates all possibilities. As he notes, "I couldn't have arranged my affairs more meticulously if I had been going to die and knew it" (135). In fact, one reason Canning gives for "writing this down" is that "in the gloom of one's own head consecutive thought is difficult" (42). And he is quite aware of his own efficient tendencies. As he says, he doesn't worry "about" the question of responsibility; he is worried "by it." The question "Whose fault is this?" goes off in his head "once a day anyway," and "the next ten minutes is a hell of muddled thinking which gets stopped only by the telephone ringing or the fact that our plates are clean. . . . It is very likely only the habit of trying to be efficient that I learned in business which makes me want to lance these boils myself, get them cleaned up and out of the way as if they interfered with my output. (What output, for God's sake?) I am not, I think, tormented by guilt" (29−30). Ironically, of course, the very automatism that has created the situation he is trying to understand governs his methodical attempts to understand it.

A Sense of Completion

This efficiency phobia that Seager bestows upon Canning does allow for one very satisfying consequence. Canning's first-person narration produces a sense of completion, a feeling that one has been led resolutely through stages of preparation, expectation, and fulfillment. One good example is the manner in which Canning approaches the fact of Hedwig's lesbianism and his own inadequate response to that knowledge. After working up to his disastrous wedding night and disclosing the fact that Hedwig did not get out of bed for twelve years, Canning searches for the reasons he did not divorce Hedwig, and he finds, among others, his grandparents, who lived for years in a bisected farmhouse and "didn't speak to each other except on domestic business" (44), his desire not to look like a fool, vague religious emotions, and his very environment. The last Canning illustrates with the anecdote of Elmer Walsey and Fred Hackendorf. This fifth-grade encounter with sadomasochistic tendencies suggests Hugh's ever inadequate preparation for the abnormal: "Perhaps I was naive or perhaps I live in a part of the country where people act straightforwardly most of the time but this was my first meeting with anything sickly, devious, and strange in human behavior, and I didn't see much of this sort of thing until I got married. I was not well prepared" (47).

Still, Canning is not satisfied. He must underscore the extent of his innocence by mentioning the many pounds of bonbons and the psychiatrist, by revealing his own patience and hope even as Hedwig begins to avenge herself upon him, hope that someday Hedwig would bear his children, "two boys and a dear little girl." Canning must stop short of the final revelation even as he recounts Hedwig's explanation—how she loved a girl, and how she came to marry Hugh. Before he can present the bare truth he tells the story of "Miss Candace Weatherby, spinster, eighty-eight years old" who "fell drunk the length of her staircase and killed herself" (53). Her behavior—the purchase of one bottle of whiskey at a time—and the manner of her death are odd, but Canning has had no difficulty understanding them. "The point if that it is a familiar oddity, and, though not unexpected, a familiar catastrophe. Not that old ladies fall drunk down their staircases very often, but it is nevertheless the kind of thing people do here. I understand it at once. I can give reasons for it" (54). Thus Canning slowly but inexorably increases the reader's understanding of the town, of both his and Hedwig's heritage and of the complex forces that have immobilized his will.

It is this incremental effect, this layering of anecdotes, that builds an effective network of foreshadowings and echoes, that, in fact, produces the sense of a patterned structure underpinning *Death of Anger*. Contained within Canning's account of the war, for example, and the effect the war had upon his relationship with Hedwig, is the anecdote of the frozen man, the twenty-three-year-old sergeant who, unable to cope with conditions, becomes "incapable of movement" (24). The sergeant's physical condition parallels Canning's own psychological condition, immobilized by forces he is unable to control.

And the recurring mention of Hugh's desire for a normal family life, especially for a son, adequately prepares for the introduction of Donald after the essential information about Hedwig has been disclosed. Even as Hedwig is in the process of disclosing her "unnatural" nature, Hugh asks her if she ever thought of having a son. The question hardly stands out in this dialogue between Hugh and Hedwig, but its importance is disclosed in the very next section which introduces Donald. Hedwig has declared that her problem is identity—Hugh has destroyed her very self, robbed her of her identity. Naturally his mind would then turn to Donald because with Donald three essential elements of the dialogue between Canning and Hedwig merge: Canning's desire for a son, eccentric behavior which the town doesn't condone because it can't understand it, and the question of identity. Once again Canning is denied a son, once again he is confronted with behavior beyond his understanding, and once again he attempts to destroy a person's identity—with the same innocence and good intentions he brought to the first fiasco. However, all three elements are double-edged in the meeting with Donald: Hugh's motives for wanting a son are exposed as petty ("immortality through property"), his own behavior is rejected as unnatural by Donald, and his identity is assaulted ("that bastard Hugh Canning").

True to the logical and incremental method, Canning begins the next section with a comment on identity: "My intentions were uncluttered by the compulsion that some men have who use business as an arena where they can discover their own identities. I was wrong, but I thought I already knew who I was, thus my intentions were really quite pure" (79).

Small Matters, Large Implications

Small matters, as well as the larger points of inquiry—such as intentions, identity, and motives—are given this treatment. In Canning's first French lessons reside both the motives for choosing that country for his flight and a foreshadowing of the ultimate nature of the trip: Mrs. Walsh's confidence that he will someday go there and the long pale finger dripping blood on the French verbs. It is indicative of Seager's craftsmanship that the bloody finger is appropriate within the anecdote itself. Isolated, it seems heavy-handed as a portent, but it is really quite subtle. As with all of Seager's symbols, it functions first and foremost as a satisfying part of the narrative.

Chance remarks, as well, take on a good deal of import in retrospect. When Donald comes to plant trees, a part of his argument with Canning stands out: "Once he confessed that he wouldn't mind having money to travel. 'But that defeats your whole offer doesn't it? I can't go tooling around France or Spain and work in your factory, can I?' he said" (129). The remark is one more example of Seager's exquisitely careful preparation for and foreshadowing of each event. That Donald specifically mentions France, of course, anticipates his journey to France as well as the double irony of his death; he does, after all, earn the money to reach France by working nights in Canning's factory. It serves a perfectly natural function in the narrative, too, strengthening the likelihood that Donald met Flora as he planted trees for Canning. The seeming innocence of Donald's statement masks the possibility that he already knows Hugh and Flora's plans, a possibility strengthened when Flora later reveals that Donald got their itinerary from Harry Wilbur—who, in fact, didn't have their itinerary.

Seager's art extends the ordinary and the seemingly inconsequential, and it does so subtly and artfully. It is perfectly natural that the anecdote of Mrs. Walsh, Donald's chance (or calculated) remark, and Hugh's revelation that he studied French in the office have the reader well prepared for the fact that he and Flora will be journeying to France. The added information, after his destination is revealed, that he didn't learn much French—"barely enough to order a meal or taxi. I think I did it to convince myself that I was going" (135)—seems proper. It also strengthens the scene with the French policeman after Donald's death, but it does more. First, it complements the moment when Hugh must face Donald in France:" *'Fine maison s'il vous plait.'* I had just been talking English to the barman. Why can't we act with dignity" (169). Second, and of more import to the weighty matters in the novel, it is one of the many ironical reinforcements of the web of circumstances that seems to have so bound Hugh Canning. Hugh's mistranslation of the guidebook at Les Baux buttresses Flora's romantic conclusion that Donald has died for her sake: " 'You see? That woman died for love,' as if a suicide way the hell off in the Middle Ages justified everything" (182). Finally, the futility of Hugh's intentions is demonstrated when he takes French lessons from the Comtesse de Rochefort, since he thought he was going to live in France (186). This final reference to French lessons caps the whole business quite effectively; once again the sense of futility and finality that pervades the novel is reinforced. Once again Hugh's intentions are meaningless when viewed in retrospect. Throughout the novel intentions prove virtually meaningless; Hugh is ever judged by his actions.

Consider, then, the futility of Hugh's concern with intentions: "As I write this, I remember he once told me he hated cars. Is that why I offered mine to him?" (171). Whatever Hugh's intentions, conscious or subconscious, Donald died in Hugh's car and complying with Hugh's request that he drive to the Riviera for a day.

The automobile is one of the best examples of the economical and masterly manner in which Seager has interlocked his motifs in *Deaths of Anger*. The automobile is, as Donald makes clear, central to the technology destroying the quality of modern life. It is linked as well to Canning's identity: Donald identifies and dislikes Canning, even before he knows him, through his Cadillac and the way he drives it slowly through the streets. Ironically, Donald "escapes" Hugh's world on land that was once Henry Ford's. Obviously it is no accident that Donald shows up in France when Canning has gone to change his car's oil, or that Hugh's business is connected to the automobile industry.

What care and exactitude on Seager's part are demonstrated in the small bit of information that Flora's father acquired his broken pelvis in an automobile accident. This accident, after all, seems to have contributed to Flora's promiscuous sexual behavior, and she herself suggests that she became a nurse because it seemed a natural thing to do after taking care of her father for so long (123). And it is as a nurse that she meets Canning. It is this interweaving of chance events, large and small, that has drawn a net of circumstance tightly around Hugh Canning.

The role of the automobile is much larger than these few examples imply. There is "the silly business of the *rond-point* in Paris," Charlie Kellerman and the German woman with the white Mercedes, Hugh's dead battery after his affair with the German woman, the drunken Johnny who enticed coeds with his "big yellow Stutz Roadster" in college, *badinage* between Hugh and Flora about the Cadillac; any of these can be examined and its place in the web that caught Hugh Canning discovered. That Hugh's parking place at the factory has only the understated sign, *Mr. Canning*, contributes to our understanding of his nature; yet, all these details, this accumulation of things automotive, are vehicles carrying weightier implications.

The manner in which Seager employs the automobile to illustrate the small beginnings that somehow have frightful endings is but one example of the craftsmanship he demonstrates in *Death of Anger*. If it is nothing else, it is a well-written novel. It has none of the loose ends of his first four novels, and perhaps this makes it less rich. It is just here, where technique has been made to serve the ends of the author and serve them inflexibly, that *Death of Anger* may have gone wrong. His first four novels have ragged edges, but those ragged edges were indicative of Seager's conception of human nature: rich, complex, impossible to pin down completely, impossible to trim all the edges for a perfect fit. In *Death of Anger* humanity is planed smooth; all the novel's seams are tight. Consequently, there is no outlet for the human spirit that the earlier novels by their very natures suggest cannot be adequately contained; they capture the nature of the human spirit, while the last novel confines the spirit. *Death of Anger* seems, in fact, to mirror the fate of its protagonist; it is bound by its own constraints. Though Seager's skill as a writer is admirably displayed in *Death of Anger* and his craft is beyond question, that very craft is, at times, disconcerting. It is as if Seager's will is at the mercy of his art, as if his options have been eliminated by the demands of his craft. The feeling is understandable, since it does reflect Seager's state of mind at the time he was writing *Death of Anger*, but it is nonetheless disturbing. Perhaps his intention did not wither in the event, for clearly he meant *Death of Anger* to be disturbing.

Chapter Eight
Nonfiction

Allan Seager wrote three nonfiction books: *They Worked For a Better World*, biographies of five important Americans; *Memoirs of a Tourist*, a translation of Stendahl's *Mémoires d'un Touriste*, slightly condensed; and *The Glass House: The Life of Theodore Roethke*. He wrote a handful of book reviews and articles as well, and these are interesting primarily as they illuminate his fiction.

Articles and Reviews

Seager wrote more articles immediately following the publication of *Amos Berry* than at any other time in his life. He clearly wanted to impose the themes of that book upon readers, and since the novel didn't reach a large audience, he tried alternate routes. "Our Dream of Comfort" appeared in *The Nation* in 1953, and it condenses the themes of *Amos Berry* into four explicit pages. His review article, "Executive Suite: The Power and the Prize," rehashed his *Amos Berry* concerns a year later, again in *The Nation*, as did "Casting Out the Tory" in 1955—at the same time it paid deference to George Orwell, a writer Seager greatly admired. And one wonders whether he reviewed Harvey Swados's *On The Line* because Swados was a friend and former student, or because of that novel's concern with the meaningless nature of work for most Americans.

Seager's articles are always interesting, whatever their concern. His examination of Arthur Miller's creative process for *Esquire*, "The Creative Agony of Arthur Miller," offers penetrating insights into Miller's methods and plays, but even here one finds echoes of Seager's fiction. Two articles written at the request of *The Nation*'s editors examine University of Michigan students a decade apart: 1957 and 1967. The 1957 students are treated roughly; they are "dull and earnest," "trained but not educated," and concerned with material acquisitions. Seager is gentler with the students of the 1960s, who have "a great store of idealism," but he doubts that they can do more than rebel, because to revolt "would be like the fish revolting against the sea."

Seager's ability to adapt to his audience is illustrated by two sports articles written thirty years apart. "How Good is Joe Louis" for *Dime*

Sport in 1935 (under the pseudonym H. W. Fordyce, the name he gave the police when he was arrested in Memphis) is simplistic, but even here Seager displays some psychoanalysis—trying to educate his audience as usual—as he tries to account for Louis's deadly manner in the ring. And in "The Precocious Champions" for *Holiday* in 1964 he declares that "moral stamina" is the essential training change enabling twelve-year-old girls to swim the 400 meters faster than Johnny Weismuller did in the 1924 Olympic Games: "The poise that comes from having known pain, exhaustion and acclaim . . . is not a bad thing for any nation." Thus he justifies somewhat the puritanical zeal with which Americans have turned "a pleasant sport into a grim novitiate of the will."

They Worked For A Better World

They Worked For A Better World is a charming book, written as part of a "notable" experiment in adult education, the Peoples Library. The American Association for Adult Education issued a series of books "at once interesting, authoritative, and not too long and difficult to read" with the help of a grant from the Carnegie Corporation in the 1930s and early 1940s. The "purposive idea" of the series, "that knowledge needs to be humanized so that ordinary citizens who are the ones who need it most in our time, may find it understandable and useful" coincided with Seager's beliefs.[1]

Seager's increasing desire to improve the quality of life for Americans probably deprived him of a loftier position in the hierarchy of American letters; indeed, he suspected as much. In his serious fiction Seager refused to write for critics or other writers. He wanted badly to reach "the ordinary citizens," to affect their lives. *They Worked For A Better World* is instantly recognizable as part of the basic pattern of Seager's life; it testifies to his desire to educate, as do his Oxford letters to his father, the swimming lessons he gave in Memphis, his willingness to lead a Great Books discussion group, the numerous aspiring writers he guided, and, indeed, his entire career at Michigan. Seager was serious about educating people; it was an essential step if the quality of life were to be raised in the Midwest, if the will were to remain free.

So he put aside the novel he was so determined to write—*Equinox*—and tried to teach "those who do not read much." Seager's short biographies of Roger Williams, Thomas Paine, Ralph Waldo Emerson, Elizabeth Stanton, and Edward Bellamy met the requirements of "30,000 words in a simple style." He demonstrated, as he often did, that he could tailor his writing to fit a particular audience.

The five biographies demonstrate, as Seager's fiction tried to show, that the past does influence the present, that to understand the forces at work in the present it is important to examine the past. The five biographies are evidence that individuals can have an effect upon the world in which they live; they are portraits of the will in action. And though the book is "earnest" and intentionally "inspirational," numerous passages call Seager's fiction to mind. For these five, "there was no gap between the ideal and the realization" because "they got to work." "The greatest obstacle to action of this kind is habit. Physical habit is a blessing, but mental habits may be traps." This is *The Inheritance* simplified: "when habit controls thinking, it is usually a blight."[2] Seager declares that the knowledge of how these people went to work may come in handy if it is ever necessary to fight for these ideals and ideas again.

The few reviews that mentioned Seager (most reviewed the series as a whole) were very kind, but this was a relatively minor event in Seager's life—from his own perspective. He did what he was asked to do, and because the task appealed to him and coincided with his own impulses, he performed it well. But even before the book was published, he returned his full attention to the novel he wanted to write.

Allan Seager, Translator

Memoirs of a Tourist was a distraction. Seager broke completely from his normal routine and, in addition, he savored the special cachet of being Allan Seager, translator. He loved France, and Stendahl was one of his favorite authors—one that he taught when he had the opportunity. The book was sent out to publishers twenty times before it was finally accepted, but Seager knew it was good, and he refused to let his agent stop circulating the manuscript.

Jay McCormick, reviewing the book in the *Detroit News*, wrote that Seager seemed "the perfect man" to translate Stendahl because of "the strong resemblances between them." Even as a translator, Seager managed to write about himself. The "tourist" shares many of Seager's opinions, and in the Preface Seager notes that one of the book's strengths is the "conscious use of the fundamental artistic device of the novelist, the adoption of a fiction as a way of revealing truth." No doubt the fact that Seager shared many of Stendahl's concerns makes this such a sparkling translation. The problem, according to Seager, "was to devise a plausible English diction for one of the most French of Frenchmen and I may say I am pleased at the way it turned out."[3] Stendahl is clearly evident in this work, his mind shines through because Seager could enter it so easily.

Biography as Autobiography: *The Glass House*

The Glass House is an excellent book, and its excellence in spite of the limitations imposed upon it (the cuts demanded by Beatrice Roethke, the refusal to permit Seager to quote from Roethke's poems) represents the triumph of Seager's will. Knowing *The Glass House* was the last book he would write, his health failing and his energy rapidly depleting, Seager fought down his rebellious impulses and excised and revised. He accepted the situation, and once having accepted it, he beat the odds. His urgent desire to complete *The Glass House* at nearly any cost is understandable, for, as he said of Theodore Roethke, "Much of his life I have acted out myself."

Seager's biography of Roethke is a final justification of Seager's own life and work, for most readers who knew Seager well are struck by the degree to which this biography of the poet is an autobiography, once removed, of Allan Seager. Indeed, there are numerous authorial asides: "(In my own childhood, Michigan sugar was bluish in color and the grains stuck together in lumps. This has now been corrected. The sugar is white and cannot be told from cane.)" and "(no one has ever made anything of the light of Michigan—it deserves as much attention as the sun of Andalusia.)"[4] Occasionally the information Seager interjects is justifiable only if one considers the book to be about Seager as well. Mentioning Roethke's stay at Algeciras, Seager writes, "a town I remember not so much for the famous conferences or that it was Molly Bloom's birthplace, but rather for a magnificent chocolate hippopotamus I saw in a store window" (128).

Robert Boyers, in "The Roethke Puzzle," a review article in the *New Republic*, speaks of Seager's "undeniable identification with a great many features of Roethke's life." Boyers is absolutely right; the identification is present from the book's outset, and it is deep. Themes and concerns in the biography are analogous to those in Seager's novels. The first chapter, "Roethke's birthplace," traces the history of the Saginaw Valley from the "vague" oral history of the Indians through de Tocqueville to the Saginaw Valley of Roethke's day. The assumption Seager makes is that Roethke is a product of the valley and its history, and he implies a "mysterious inheritance" from "an earlier time" that gave Roethke "a furious energy out of proportion to what was spent around him."

Roethke inherited the energy of the first settlers, the pioneers, and somehow he escaped the pattern that grew up after the valley's lumber was gone and the violent lumberjack spirit was no longer a requirement for survival: "The pace of life slowed and became peaceful, and the lives tended to repeat themselves without much change from one generation to the next. . . . What had been discovered to be convenient ways of doing things crystallized into habits so rigid that any departure from them could be sustained by a sense of actual guilt" (7). This is virtually a paraphrase of the speech Eddie Burcham gives to Walter Phelps in Seager's second novel, *The Inheritance*. The first chapter of *The Glass House*, then, is an implementation of a theme that recurs in Seager's novels.

Roethke's childhood, detailed in chapter three, touches Seager's on a number of points: "Like so many boys in America who are intelligent and sensitive, more so than the people around them, he read beyond his years, indiscriminately, but with great concentration" (27). This was also true of Seager and of Charles Berry, poet and narrator of *Amos Berry*. Seager notes Roethke's developing sense of place (which Seager had, in his journals, noted in himself), and discussing Roethke's tendency as a young man to be "romantically, hyperbolically gloomy," he notes that "his despair seems to prove that he already had the prime requisites of a poet, a tingling sensitivity as if he lacked an outer layer of skin, and some sort of compulsion to elevate his life, his emotions into words" (28). Again, Seager could as easily have been writing about the Allan Seager of the Memphis Journals, or of his character Charles Berry.

In chapter four the parallels become more obvious and more explicit. High school courses were too easy for Roethke, but he dared not be known as an intellectual because it meant ostracism. "He was not yet old enough to criticize the society he moved in. . . . He wanted to belong" (37). Ted began to drink, which gave him "the double pleasure of simultaneous conformity and protest." This double pleasure runs through the biography, just as it ran through Seager's life. "And if the drinking and playing around with boys who were his intellectual inferiors were concessions he made to ward off their sneers, he was too young to know they were concessions. His public manner seems to have been the beginning of an effort to shield the best part of himself, to protect it from the rigors of a rough climate" (39). This is how Seager's friends explain his public mask, too.

Roethke's actions upon the death of his father suggest Walter Phelps of *The Inheritance*: "That night he took his father's place at the head of the table and he sat there from that day on" (43). So does the information that when Roethke went to Ann Arbor he was the first of his family to go to a university. This was true of Seager, too. "Even the study of literature was strange in his family. . . . It is hard to convey how strange, how foreign the wilful making of a poem would have been in a society like his, the inert weight of custom that not only did not have room for any original work in the arts but feared and hated it" (46). Again, the same was true for Seager and Charles Berry. The passage also suggests the significance Seager attached to the fact that Amos Berry had once composed a poem in his fraternity room. That act implied Amos's potential for rejecting his society.

"College," chapter five of *The Glass House*, could with very few alterations be an account of Seager's college life. Seager and Roethke attended the University of Michigan, and they were there at the same time. Since there "was no tradition of hard grinding work" at Michigan, Roethke made his own tradition, as did Seager. And while a few of the faculty members were genuinely learned, "Far too many, on the other hand, were mere specialists who had struggled up from small colleges, brandishing their degrees, arrogantly and ignorantly insisting on the importance of their study without any very clear notion of its connection with others in the field or with the great body of knowledge as a whole" (47). This is clearly Seager speaking, and it is something he had said in each of his novels. *Amos Berry* states it most explicitly, for it is this specialization, ultimately, that drives Amos to murder.

Roethke was a "snob" at college in much the same way Seager was, and he was aware of this tendency—as was Seager. He was also "kind of a pack rat" who saved most of his college lectures. Seager did the same. The tough-guy image Ted cultivated suggests the Seager who took up boxing, and like Seager, Roethke, "reconciling opposites," made Phi Beta Kappa. "He was a large man furnished with more genuine desires and appetites than most people and publicly he seemed to want to make an impression of completeness as the master of many talents, poet, scholar, athlete, chef, lover, teacher" (61). Each of these talents Seager himself displayed.

One could proceed slowly through the whole book, pulling sentence after sentence from page after page, showing that the descriptions of Roethke are quite often also descriptions of Seager—but to do so would simply be to rewrite half of *The Glass House*. Roethke liked the same jazz Seager liked. Roethke believed that literature was important, and he had the ability to convince his students that this was true. Roethke contended that "the ultimate death is the death of the will." In actuality, Roethke's ambition and willingness to work hard made him a typical middle-class American of his day. His mother's influence subtly colored his relations with women later in life. He had complete confidence in his own craftsmanship. He was classified 4-F. He began to consider himself a gourmet cook. He loved the odd detail, the strange fact: "The history books say that Allen beat on a door of the fort and intoned, 'Open in the name of God and the Continental Congress.' The local tale, however, which may have come down by word of mouth, is that Allen beat on the door and shouted, 'Open the door you goddamned British sons-of-bitches, or we'll kick it in' " (131). Roethke had a low opinion of academics. Roethke felt the Agrarians were vastly overvalued. Roethke knew he was undervalued as an artist.

The list grows longer and longer, and one can only wonder if Seager selected and emphasized those details which linked him with Roethke, or if his familiarity with the experiences worked some unconscious selection and expansion. In *The Glass House* Seager says, "All any writer has to work with is his own experience. (I do not know what critics mean when they say a poet has 'transcended his own experience')" (143). That Seager wrote "writer" rather than "poet" is telling. Not only is it another link to Roethke, but perhaps evidences his awareness that in examining Roethke's life he was examining his own. Many of the excerpts Seager pulls from Roethke's notebooks are indicative: "Make poetry the reflection of your life" and "To love objects is to love life" are pure Seager.

Why should Seager note that "the perspective afforded by Europe throws America into high relief," even though there is little evidence in Roethke's poems that this was true for him? Why mention Roethke's slow "realization that the rest of the world was as banal and inimical as Saginaw" (221), then do little with it? It seems clear that, consciously or unconsciously, Seager drew heavily on those things he and Roethke shared, leaving clues that revealed not only the poet Roethke but the writer Seager. Seager chose the following excerpt from a two-page introduction Roethke wrote to a section of the fourth edition of *New World Writing*: "He [the ordinary reader] will not be afraid of feeling—and this in spite of the deep-rooted fear of emotion existing today, particularly among the half-alive, for whom emotion, even when incorporated into form, becomes a danger, a madness. Poetry is written for the whole man. . . . " The passage deals, of course, with one of Seager's central concerns, the whole man, and he commented on it thus: "The truth of this observation seems to me to be immediately striking. A technological society like ours is based on logic. It cannot recognize emotion except as a disruptive force, and in offices, in factories, in laboratories, disruptive forces cannot be countenanced and must be repressed. Yet a man has his emotions and, repressed, they can eat him up. The 'half-alive' is Ted's recognition of those so eaten" (216).

That from two pages, Seager chose this small portion, and that he chose to comment upon it as he did and then move abruptly to minor details in his next paragraph suggests that he included these words of Roethke's because they struck a responsive chord in himself. This, after all, is Seager's diagnosis of the individual's tragedy in the modern world, "There is more to us than the life we have fashioned for ourselves will allow us to use."[5] It is a thesis in each of his novels. And in his best novel, *Amos Berry*, the concept of the whole man is not only central, it is also explicit. Charles Berry speaks of his intention to be present when his father murdered Walt Rickert: "It is not the intention that governs talk in the street or shadowboxing or wheedling hospitality out of stupid friends. It is rather the intention you hope to use in writing poetry, that of the marvelous stranger, the whole man."

Finally, in a passage Seager selects from Roethke's application for an extension of his Fulbright grant, one must consider the importance, the truth, this statement would have for Seager himself: "In twenty years of teaching I have become more and more convinced of the desirability of presenting minor writers as one of the principal clues to an age. The 'big' figures would keep coming in repeatedly by way of contrast: they would remain in the background against which one plays another music" (232-33).

Just as Seager's fiction was autobiographical, so was his nonfiction. Even writing the biography of another man, Seager wrote about himself. Indeed, his subject was always himself, and he knew it. It was part of his theory of literature, for he believed that ultimately the evaluation of an artist's work was an evaluation of the artist's life. Such a belief was not in harmony with an era that had embraced the formalist approach to literature, and that belief may well have contributed to Seager's lack of popularity.•

A summary of a speech he delivered near the end of his life (given, appropriately, at a writers conference) not only provides a glimpse of the wholeness Seager sought but also indicates the emphasis he put on the individual life. Seager noted that artists once worked "*ad majorem dei gloriam* anonymously, but they could afford to—under the feudal system they knew who they were." However, under democracy "man is what he does not how he was born." With everything now done "by groups, teams, and committees, identity is lost and not for sufficient reason. The arts are a way of identifying one's self." Hence the artist works "alone on his own terms—the last individual."

Seager ends the speech with a story an anthropologist gave him from the Marquesas Islands. After puberty rites decided which boys would be sculptors, they were placed under the tutelage of old men. Their training began with the Marquesan legends of creation: "When at last a boy was allowed to carve a figure he began to recite the legends of creation and kept it up as he worked at his carving. As it neared completion he began to name all created things, and as he gave the last touch to his own carving, he named it as the last one." Seager's analysis of the story says a great deal about his own themes, methods, and artistic theory. It explains his approach to *The Glass House*:

This little story says much. The artist's towering ego is satisfied and he has done his work in the service of something larger than himself, something he believes in utterly, his gods. If modern artists are seldom articulate about their religion, it is not that they are unbelievers. They are clearly believers in the total life of human beings. When we consider how we are cramped and stifled, how our lives are curtailed by our jobs, our habits, our lack of faith, when we consider the vast resources of Death, this is enough.[6]

Chapter Nine
"The Conscience of the Middle Class"

Allan Seager worried about the quality of life in America, and he attempted to alter it, if only in a small way, for the better. His novels, as friend and fellow novelist George Milburn put it, expose the "green rot" at the heart of the American Dream. And while they certainly do that, they do much more—they explore the reasons for the deterioration and they suggest remedies. Among the reasons is the primacy, in twentieth-century America, of organization, which has gradually become an end rather than a means. As an end, it has diminished the individual and virtually destroyed the notion of the whole man. In an age dominated by the specialization born of organization Seager was interested in the whole man.

Seager was convinced that the evolution of the novel itself was a symptom of the wrong direction the twentieth century had taken: its "focus had narrowed from a contemplation and criticism of the entire social scene to the minute examination of the psychology of its central figure."[1] Seager's critical neglect stems partly from his rejection of the focus of the modern novel. While he clearly engages in minute psychological examination of his central characters, he does so as part of a much larger contemplation and criticism of society.

As a novelist, Seager is a complex, serious thinker. He offers no easy answers, and he rejects most contemporary solutions. In fact, he suggests that many of the modern world's "solutions"—technology, the social sciences, programs of governmental care—are among the causes of the problem. The novel, he felt, reflected society's ills; it had been "broken up into dream and solipsism." *Amos Berry*, Seager's most ambitious—and probably best—novel, traces the processes that have led to this breakup, this strange and precarious balance that has been reached between the inner and outer realities. Amos Berry is a solipsist, and his personal tragedy stems from an inability to alter that fact even after he is made aware of it. "History is only what I can remember," Amos laments, and thus he speaks for most of the modern world.

Seager explores the tremendous effect that history existing beyond the memory of the individual, nevertheless, has upon the most basic aspects of daily behavior, the most trivial decisions, the very quality of life. This exploration is an integral part of the grave responsibility Seager felt as an artist. He declared in his Guggenheim application that he felt his role as a novelist was nothing less than "the conscience of the middle class."

Consequently, Seager's novels are novels of ideas. He wanted his readers to be troubled by his themes; he wanted to change their established, habitual thought patterns. He wanted to teach them. His novels deal repeatedly with people who "have more to them" than their restricted lives will let them use, and he tries, in his fiction, to help his readers discover this "more" that the modern world is "shoving down into the darkness." Again and again he explores the restraints, the forces at work in the modern world to immobilize the will. These assaulting forces are numerous, powerful, and unrelenting. Only awareness of the constraints on the will can lead to action, and only action can lead to freedom. Seager's attempt to educate the reader, his obsession with acquiring and conveying knowledge, is a valiant effort to force the reader toward awareness.

Unfortunately, Seager's works have not reached a wide audience, and his attempts have thus far been relatively futile. His neglect is undeserved, for he was a serious artist as well as a master craftsman. His fate is perhaps most poignantly illustrated by those reviewers who accused him of being seriously out of tune with his times; obviously they failed to read his novels carefully, for not only was he intentionally out of tune with his times, but he wanted also to force his readers out of tune with the worst aspects of the times.

Although a number of highly respected writers and critics—Malcolm Cowley, John Davenport, Carl Sandburg, Robert Penn Warren, Theodore Roethke, Sherwood Anderson, Hugh Kenner—have recognized Seager's talent and his worth, his place in American letters is at the very best ambiguous. Realistically, he is at present a minor writer—a nearly forgotten writer, in fact. The question of whether or not his work will, as James Dickey and Donald Hall have suggested, receive the accolades it deserves somewhere in the future can be answered only by time. The question of whether his current obscurity is deserved or lamentable is moot, to be sure. Yet Allan Seager's own reputation may well be a barometer of the modern condition: its elevation could very well depend upon a justification of Seager's "great act of faith": the rediscovery of the "more" to be found in individuals that the modern world has shoved "down into the darkness" and will not let them use.

Notes and References

Chapter One

1. Stanley Kunitz, ed., *Twentieth Century American Authors, First Supplement* (New York, 1955), pp. 889-90.
2. The Allan Seager Collection (70/176), separate volumes: v. 1, Diary, 1924-June 1925, Bancroft Library, University of California at Berkeley; hereafter this collection will be referred to as Bancroft Collection.
3. This "quote" from Job (5:7) is variously worded throughout Seager's notes, letters, and works. The words "trouble" and "darkness" are often substituted for "sorrow."
4. Separate volumes: v. 1, Diary, 1924-June 1925, Bancroft Collection.
5. Separate volumes: v. 2, Diary, June 1925-March 1926, Bancroft Collection.
6. Carton 6: School Papers, "The Scheme of *Ulysses*," Bancroft Collection.
7. Separate volumes: v. 3, Diary, March 1926-August 1927, Bancroft Collection.
8. Letter, typed; Seager to his father, November 16 [1930], Bancroft Collection.
9. Hugh Whitney Morrison to his mother, January 26, 1932; photocopy transmitted to this author by Mr. Morrison from original in his possession.
10. Seager to Helen Rudolphi Tremble, March 20, 1923.
11. Seager to his father, October 23, 1933 and February 24, 1934, Bancroft Collection.
12. Seager to Edmund Blunden, May 6, 1935, at Humanities Research Center, University of Texas at Austin.
13. Hugh Kenner to this author, March 27, 1973.
14. Seager to Jane Sherman Lehac, October 8, 1935.
15. Seager to Lehac, November 4, 1935.
16. Seager to Lehac, October 8, 1935.
17. Josh Greenfeld to this author, June 6, 1973.
18. Box 5: Diary Notes, 1931-1960, "Bennington, Vermont 1944," Bancroft Collection.
19. Box 5: Diary Notes, 1931-1960, "February, no, March 3, 1953," Bancroft Collection.
20. Box 5: Diary Notes, 1931-1960, "The Trip, September 10, 1956," Bancroft Collection.
21. Seager to Knox Burger, February 19, 1963.
22. Letter, February 13, 1973, from Joan Seager Fry to this author.
23. Hugh Kenner to this author, March 27, 1973.
24. Joan Fry to this author, March 25, 1973.

Chapter Two

1. Seager to Helen Rudolphi Tremble, October 29, 1934.
2. Allan Seager, *The Old Man of the Mountain* (New York, 1950); hereafter page references are cited in the text.
3. Seager to Horace Schwartz, June 10, 1953, Bancroft Collection.
4. Hugh Kenner, "The Insider," *Critique: Studies in Modern Fiction* 2 (Winter 1959): 3-15.
5. Box 5: Diary Notes, 1931-1960, Bancroft Collection.
6. Kenner, "The Insider," p. 5.
7. Allan Seager, "Command Performance," *Vanity Fair* 43 (November 1934): 66.
8. Box 5: Diary Notes, 1931-1960, "October 3, [1950]," Bancroft Collection.
9. James Korges, "Curiosities: Nin and Miller, Hemingway and Seager," *Critique: Studies in Modern Fiction* 7 (Spring/Summer 1965): 80.
10. Allan Seager, *A Frieze of Girls: Memoirs as Fiction* (New York, 1964), hereafter cited in the text as *FOG* followed by page number.

Chapter Three

1. Seager to Jane Sherman Lehac, April 17, 1939.
2. Seager to Jane Sherman Lehac, March 11, 1936.
3. Kenner, "The Insider," pp. 3-15.
4. Allan Seager, *Equinox* (New York, 1943), 3; hereafter page references are given in parentheses in the text.
5. Allan Seager Manuscripts, Box 2, Item 3, Working Notebook for *Equinox*, holograph, Mugar Memorial Library, Boston University.

Chapter Four

1. Seager's 1965 Guggenheim application form, Bancroft Collection.
2. Kunitz, *Twentieth Century*, pp. 889-90.
3. Joan Fry to this author, February 6, 1973.
4. Richard Match, "Mapled Streets," *New York Herald Tribune Book Review*, June 20, 1948, p. 8.
5. Phrases in Seager letter to Horace Schwartz, June 10, 1953.
6. Allan Seager, *The Inheritance* (New York, 1948), p. 1; hereafter page references are given in parentheses in the text.
7. Box 5: Diary Notes, 1931-1960, "November 15, 1945," Bancroft Collection.
8. Daniel Boorstin, *The Image or What Happened to the American Dream?* (New York: Atheneum, 1962), *passim.*
9. Seager quotes this variously. See page 94 of *The Glass House*, "The ultimate death is the death of the will." The variations would appear to be Seager's rather than Roethke's.

Chapter Five

1. Seager to Horace Schwartz, June 10, 1953.
2. Seager to Earl Karr, December 15, 1954.
3. Allan Seager, *Amos Berry* (New York, 1953), p. 91; hereafter page references are given in parentheses in the text.
4. Author's interview with James Goodrich; Onsted, Michigan, Summer 1973.
5. John Brooks, "Muddled Nemesis," *New York Times*, March 1, 1953, p. 30.
6. Seager to Schwartz, June 10, 1953.

Chapter Six

1. James Kelly, "Troubled Pastures," *New York Times Book Review*, July 22, 1956, pp. 4, 12.
2. Allan Seager, *Hilda Manning* (New York, 1956), p. 145; hereafter page references are given in parentheses in the text.
3. Seager's personal notes in possession of Joan Fry.

Chapter Seven

1. Typescript (1974) in possession of Joan Fry.
2. Allan Seager, *Death of Anger* (New York, 1960), p. 213; hereafter page references are given in parentheses in the text.

Chapter Eight

1. Raymond G. Fuller, "Knowledge Humanized," *Saturday Review of Literature*, May 27, 1939, p. 18.
2. Allan Seager, *They Worked for a Better World* (New York, 1939), p. 6.
3. Guggenheim application, Bancroft Collection.
4. Allan Seager, *The Glass House: The Life of Theodore Roethke* (New York, 1968), pp. 6, 32; hereafter page references are given in parentheses in the text.
5. Seager to Schwartz, June 10, 1953.
6. Seager's personal notes; examined and copied by the present author, Summer 1974; originals in possession of Joan Fry.

Chapter Nine

1. The rough draft of notes Seager meant to send someone on *The Growth of American Literature*, Bancroft Collection.

Selected Bibliography

PRIMARY SOURCES

1. *Books*
Novels
Amos Berry. New York: Simon and Schuster, 1953.
Death of Anger. New York: McDowell, Obolensky, 1960.
Equinox. New York: Simon and Schuster, 1943.
Hilda Manning. New York: Simon and Schuster, 1956.
The Inheritance. New York: Simon and Schuster, 1948.

Short Stories
A Frieze of Girls: Memoirs as Fiction. New York: McGraw-Hill, 1964.
The Old Man of The Mountain. New York: Simon and Schuster, 1950.

Nonfiction
The Glass House: The Life of Theodore Roethke. New York: McGraw-Hill, 1968.
They Worked for a Better World. New York: Macmillan, 1939.

Translation
Memoirs of a Tourist. Evanston: Northwestern University Press, 1962. (from
  Stendahl's *Memoires d'un Touriste)*

2. *Short Stories*
"Actress With Red Garters." *Esquire* 52 (December 1959); 337-45.
"Another Man's Wife." *Saturday Evening Post,* October 14, 1961, pp. 46-48,
  50, 52.
"The Arab Pilot." *Michigan Alumni Quarterly Review* 67 (Winter 1961):
  138-42.
"As a Little Child." *Esquire* 11 (December 1939): 65, 168-70.
"The Astonished Mr. Drummond." *Good Housekeeping* 144 (March 1957):
  84-85, 178, 180, 182, 184-85.
"The Bang on the Head." *Good Housekeeping* 123 (August 1946): 37, 80-85.
"Berkshire Comedy." *Story* 12 (May 1938): 9-15.
"Charity Begins." *Vanity Fair* 45 (January 1936): 26-27, 62.
"A City for Cavalry." *First Person* 1 (Fall 1960): 26-31.
"Colorless in Limestone Caverns." *Playboy* 15 (November 1969): 109, 114,
  190.

"Command Performance." *Vanity Fair* 43 (November 1934): 29, 66.
"The Conqueror." *Story* 26 (January-February 1945): 50-61.
"The Cousin to the Emperor." *Vanity Fair* 44 (June 1935): 28, 58.
"The Cure." *Atlantic* 213 (February 1964): 62-68.
"Dear Old Shrine Our Hearts Round Thee Twine." *Esquire* 54 (December 1960): 301-8.
"The Drinking Contest." *Esquire* 56 (December 1961): 127, 244, 247-48, 250-51.
"The Drunkard's Wife." *Collier's,* August 6, 1949, pp. 26, 34, 36-37.
"The Enchanted Princess." *San Francisco Review* 1 (March 1961): 67-76.
"The Fellow From Puyricard." *Michigan Alumni Quarterly Review* 63 (Spring 1957): 235-38.
"The Fixer." *Collier's,* September 25, 1937, pp. 42, 44-45.
"Fugue for Harmonicas." *Vanity Fair* 44 (March 1935): 32, 64.
"Game Chickens." *Foreground* 1 (Spring 1946): 126, 140.
"The Good Doctor." *Playboy* 12 (March 1966): 99, 154-55.
"The Great Turtle Migration." *Michigan Alumni Quarterly Review*, 64 (Autumn 1958): 59-60.
"The Half Dollar With the Hole in it and the Little Candy Hearts." *Esquire* 48 (September 1957): 118.
"Her Only Son." *Saturday Evening Post*, February 2, 1957, pp. 30, 56-58, 60.
"The Honest Husband." *Redbook* 117 (September 1961): 42, 99-101.
"I'll Marry You in Church." *Cosmopolitan* 129 (August 1950): 33, 89-96.
"Image-Breaker." *Vanity Fair* 45 (November 1935): 21, 62-63.
"The Innocent Captive." *Saturday Evening Post*, November 12, 1958, pp. 37, 68, 73-74.
"The Intruder." *Good Housekeeping* 143 (November 1956): 66-88, 162-64, 166-68, 170, 172-74, 176.
"It's Hard to Recognize a Drowning Man." *Esquire* 49 (March 1958): 63-64.
"I Want a Divorce." *Saturday Evening Post*, September 29, 1956, pp. 26, 130-34.
"Jersey, Guernsey, Alderney, Sark." *Esquire* 16 (August 1941): 40, 120-21.
"A Journey Home." *Vanity Fair* 45 (September 1935): 26, 57.
"The Joys of Sport at Oxford." *Sports Illustrated*, October 29, 1962, pp. 60-69.
"Lazarus." *Vanity Fair* 43 (January 1935): 21, 60.
"Love Dance." *Cosmopolitan* 144 (March 1958): 107-11.
"The Marriage Wrecker." *Saturday Evening Post.* March 1, 1958, pp. 23, 62, 65.
"Mary Vincent and the Convict." *Good Housekeeping* 138 (January 1954): 60-61, 191.
"The Mesdames Kilbourne." *Vanity Fair* 46 (February 1936): 25, 64.
"The Mink Stole." *Good Housekeeping* 121 (August 1945): 32-33, 70-76, 78-79.
"Miss Anglin's Bad Martini." *Esquire* 56 (September 1961): 86-88, 90, 160-62.

"The Musical Saw and Pygmalion the Less." *Spectrum* 1 (Spring-Summer 1957): 33-41.
"The Nicest Girl in Cook County." *New Yorker*, September 15, 1956, pp. 42-47.
"No More Roses." *Saturday Evening Post*, March 27, 1965, pp. 52-58.
"No Son, No Gun, No Streetcar." *Harper's Bazaar* 82 (March 1948): 204, 300, 302.
"The Old Goat." *Collier's*, April 5, 1952, pp. 25, 60-62.
"One Jaguar Shot Dead." *Esquire* 128 (March 1961): 67-69.
"One Kind Deed." *Popular*, April, 1937, p. 101.
"One More Hero." *Cosmopolitan* 128 (February 1950): 62, 64, 107-11.
"The Pictures." *Good Housekeeping* 124 (February 1947): 22, 124.
"Politeness." *Michigan Alumni Quarterly Review* 64 (Autumn 1958): 60-63.
"Pommery, 1921." *Vanity Fair* 43 (October 1934): 43-65.
"Powder River in the Old Days." *New Yorker*, August 17, 1957, pp. 28-34.
"Pro Arte." *Scribner's Magazine* 101 (February 1937): 31-37.
"Pursuit." *Cosmopolitan* 130 (May 1951): 30, 151-58.
"The Romantic Life of Harper Galloway." *Good Housekeeping* 119 (September 1944): 20-21, 61-62, 64, 67, 69-72, 74.
"The Rope." *Atlantic* 215 (January, 1965): 79-82.
"Sacrament." *Vanity Fair* 43 (December 1934): 22, 70.
"Second Wedding." *Good Housekeeping* 128 (May 1949): 46-47, 117-26.
"The Shadow on the Wall: A Folktale." *Generation* 10 (Spring 1959): 46.
"Shock Treatment." *Saturday Evening Post*, April 12, 1958, pp. 27, 67-68, 70.
"Slow Train to Brussels." *Vanity Fair* 43 (December 1934): 22, 70.
"The Street." *Vanity Fair* 43 (September 1934): 36, 62.
"A Taste of Champagne." *Cosmopolitan* 144 (January 1958): 99-100, 102-3.
"Under the Big Magnolia Tree." *New Yorker*, March 20, 1954, pp. 35-40.
"Virtue Preserved, or the Visit of Great Uncle Martin." *Vanity Fair* 45 (December 1935): 46, 61.
"A Whole Hundred Points Against." *Story* 33 (1960): 170-77.

3. *Articles*
"Casting Out the Tory." *The Nation*, November 5, 1955, pp. 396-97.
"The Class of '67: The Gentle Desperadoes." *The Nation*, June 19, 1967, p. 778.
"The Creative Agony of Arthur Miller." *Esquire* 52 (October 1959): 123-26.
"Executive Suite: The Power and the Prize." *The Nation*, December 11, 1954, pp. 506-8.
"Inside the Machine." *The Nation*, November 23, 1957, p. 393.
"Michigan." *The Nation*, March 9, 1957, pp. 206-7.
"Our Dream of Comfort." *The Nation*, December 12, 1953, pp. 519-22.
"Oxford: What's it Like." *University* 1, no. 2 (n.d.): 16-18, 73.
"The Precocious Champions." *Holiday* 35 (June 1964); 110, 138-41.

"Symposium on the Teaching of Creative Writing." *Four Quarters* 10 (January 1961): 16.

4. The Allan Seager Collection (70/176) of the Bancroft
   Library, University of California at Berkeley

The Bancroft's Seager Collection is extensive and invaluable.

Among the holdings:
    Correspondence
    Diaries and Diary Notes
    Manuscripts, typescripts, and galleys of the books.
    Short Stories: published and unpublished
    Articles: published and unpublished
    School Papers
    Miscellaneous Personalia

SECONDARY SOURCES

1. Bibliography
Hanna, Allan. "An Allan Seager Bibliography." *Critique: Studies in Modern Fiction* 3 (Winter 1962-63): 37-61. An annotated checklist of writing by and about Seager from 1934 through 1962.

2. Biographical and Critical Essays
Baker, Sheridan. "On the Diagonal." *Michigan Quarterly Review* 8 (Winter 1969): 1-2. An informative and perceptive memorial essay by a colleague who knew Seager.
Bloom, Robert. "Allan Seager: Some Versions of Disengagement." *Critique: Studies in Modern Fiction* 3 (Winter 1962-63): 4-26. Examines the typical protagonists of Seager novels, with extended discussions of *Equinox* and *The Inheritance*.
Dickey, James. "The Greatest American Poet." *Atlantic*, 222 (November 1968): 280-82. Primarily about Roethke, but discusses Seager and the strong identification Dickey feels with Charles Berry of *Amos Berry*.
Hanna, Allan. "The Muse of History: Allan Seager and the Criticism of Culture." *Critique: Studies in Modern Fiction* 3 (Winter 1962-63): 37-61. Deals with the emphasis Seager has placed on ideas in his fiction and the manner in which he has probed American culture in the twentieth century.
Kenner, Hugh. "The Insider." *Critique: Studies in Modern Fiction* 1 (Winter 1959): 3-15. The best examination and explication of Seager's work to date. Notes his seriousness, his talent, and his typical method.

Kunitz, Stanley, ed. *Twentieth Century Authors, First Supplement*. New York: American Book Company, 1951, pp. 377-78. A brief biographical sketch, including comments by Seager.

Lid, R.W. "The Innocent Eye." *Critique: Studies in Modern Fiction* 3 (Winter 1962-63): 62-74. Notes that Seager has studied the manners of midland America. Discusses Seager's typical "doubling" of characters and his characteristic use of detail.

Quigley, Genevieve L. *Michigan Quarterly Review* 9 (Fall 1970): 247-51. A charming and perceptive essay in biography. Captures the complex character of Seager: Tecumseh resident, university professor, cook, writer, and friend.

Webster, Harvey Curtis. "Seager as a Social Novelist." *Critique: Studies in Modern Fiction* 3 (Winter 1962-63): 27-36. Deals primarily with the novels and the manner in which Seager explores the betrayal of the American dream in contemporary America.

Index